THE ROBIN

THE ROBIN

Mike Read, Martin King
and Jake Allsop

BLANDFORD

Paperback first published in the U.K. 1995
by Cassell plc
Wellington House
125 Strand
London WC2R 0BB

Previously published in hardback 1992

Distributed in the United States by
Sterling Publication Co., Inc.
387 Park Avenue South, New York, N.Y. 10016–8810

Distributed in Australia by
Capricorn Link (Australia) Pty Ltd.
2/13 Carrington Road, Castle Hill, NSW 2154

British Library Cataloguing-in-Publication Data.
A catalogue record for this book is available from the British Library

ISBN 0-7137-2584-2

Typeset by Litho Link Ltd, Welshpool, Powys, Wales.
Printed and bound in Hong Kong by Dah Hua Printing Press Co. Ltd.

Contents

Acknowledgements

We have mentioned in the text some of the people who helped us in various ways. Among them we should like to single out the following: John Morgan, for wise counsel, solid information and for letting us interrupt his ringing; and Paul Mason, for providing us with two stuffed birds and also some nice snippets of information. They, and Paul Prior, read through the manuscript and made useful suggestions. Jeremy Sorensen provided data on breeding robins at Minsmere. Many other people not mentioned in the book made contributions to our studies and photography. We thank them all, and in particular Kay Kenrick, Patrick Carden, Norman Hutchinson and Valerie Thurston for allowing us unrestricted access to the robins in their gardens. We acknowledge Robert Gross, who took the excellent photograph of the fishing robin; and Dennis Bright, whose photograph of the juvenile robin sunbathing was supplied through Swift Picture Library. We also thank Robert Gillmor who drew the pictures of a developing chick on page 77. Thanks should also go to Carlton Cards Ltd. for their permission for us to use card artwork by Audrey North and to Webb Ivory for allowing us to include a number of their card designs.

Finally, we would like to thank Liz Read for her moral and practical support, and for prodding us into action at times when we were inclined to flag.

Introduction

The robin is a familiar bird and it is a splendid bird, a creature of great character and individuality. When you think of the wonderful chromatic plumage of macaws, the iridescence of sunbirds or the fantastic feathering of Mandarin ducks, you might wonder why anyone should want to devote himself single-mindedly to a photographic study of a bird which, by contrast, is relatively plain and ordinary to look at. The answer is not hard to find. We have never met anyone who did not have a good, affectionate word for the robin. Gardeners love the robin, people who put out food for the birds love the robin. Even that hardened race, the twitchers, whose sole aim in life seems to be to see every new and rare species of bird that strays to these shores, will admit that it is impossible not to notice a robin standing perkily on a fence-post or singing from a twig. For us, in our various incarnations as birdwatchers, British Trust for Ornithology census-takers, ringers or photographers, the robin had long been a part of our lives, and we were delighted to be given a chance to get to know it better.

The truth of the matter is that the robin is no ordinary bird. After all, what bird *is* 'ordinary' once you really get to know it? As we watched robins through the cycle of their lives – fighting and feeding, mating and breeding, singing and sighing (well, that's how their subsong sounds to us) – we began to realize how full of character the robin is. Nor are we the first to have found that out. Here is a quotation from a Victorian writer on birds' eggs and nests:

> I remember throwing a stone at a Robin when a very little boy, and to my consternation and utter grief, no less than to my surprise, killing it. I 'felt bad' about it – as our American friends say – and thought I was as wicked as the Sparrow of bow-and-arrow memory.
>
> It seems to be, or to have been a common feeling among boys, and is embodied in the old lines:
> The Robin and the Wren
> Are God's Cock and Hen.

The writer, a clergyman called Reverend Atkinson, also wonders how others can be so indifferent to the robin's beauty as to regard it primarily as something for the pot: 'This amiable little songster is eaten roasted with bread crumbs' (from a French recipe, also quoted by Dr David Lack in his classic work *The Life of the Robin*).

Wherever we look, the robin is described – except in French recipes, that is – in terms of the greatest affection and respect, a reflection of its close involvement with the life and doings of man. This association must have started long ago when the practice of coppicing was at its height, for coppiced woodland was – and still is – the favoured breeding habitat of the robin. Later it spread to farmland hedgerows and on to churchyards, parks and finally into our gardens and allotments. Thus, for centuries, from woodcutters to amateur gardeners, we have been a friend to and befriended by the robin. This close association with human beings and their habitations is attested time and again in the correspondence we have received from friends who knew what we were up to:

> The little devil spent the whole winter in our conservatory, and we finally had to drive it out when Spring came or it would never have bothered to find a mate! [Keith Gipp, Haddenham, Ely]

> I tamed them (with a little bit of cheese!) to sit on my fingers when I weeded the garden. I used to whistle to them at breakfast time and they would come and perch on top of the coal bunker and have cheese, cut-up raisins and crushed nuts. [Mollie Mason, Ferndown, Dorset]

> When I returned, my wife told me about the robin perching on the bottom of her bed and 'talking' to her before flying out of the bedroom, down the stairs and to the hall, through the kitchen, and out. [Geoffrey Pett, Verwood, Dorset]

Mrs Pett's observation follows a respectable literary tradition, for the poet Wordsworth mentioned in a footnote to his poem 'The Redbreasts' that, when his sister Dorothy was ill, a robin came regularly to her room and:

> used to sing and fan her face with its wings in a manner most touching.

Another nice domestic touch comes from the New Forest:

> They came regularly into the house for sultanas and cheese, and one day, one of them flew around the house before ending up in the bathroom. He flew out of the window and within minutes was back again for his cheese. [Joan Webster, Burley, Hampshire]

10

If those references to raisins (chopped-up, too — such dedication!), cheese and sultanas suggest that the robin's love for man is of the cupboard variety, it is still a remarkable relationship when you truly feel that the bird is 'talking' to you from the foot of your bed. Sometimes, as with all friends, there are sharp moments too:

> One day, we went in and heard a lot of chirping so we knew that the eggs had hatched, but when we went in after that, we got such a surprise. As soon as we put our head in the door, there was a flurry of wings and a nasty peck on the head, so if my husband wanted anything from the shed, it was a race against being dive-bombed! [Mrs Iris Wells, Ferndown, Dorset]

Even better is this gem:

> To cut a long story short, we honestly went into that shed with a crash helmet and a pair of motor-cycle goggles on!!! Anyone who dared to venture to go near their nest was instantly attacked.

It gets still more exciting:

> If I had to be in the shed for a while, I had to shut them out completely as they would peck me on my face and scratch with their needle-like claws; on one occasion my son and his friend . . . were attacked *outside* the shed and his friend fled up the garden path!

Thank you, George Cox of Ringwood, Hampshire, for these descriptions: your reference to 'needle-like claws' gives a nice dramatic touch to the event.

This book, then, is our account of the photographic study we made of robins through various stages of their lives. We have tried in the text to support our photography with interesting and thought-provoking information about the robin. If, as you read the book and look at the pictures, you find that the focus shifts occasionally from the bird to the observers, regard it as a confirmation of the fact that our lives and the lives of the robins which we studied became inextricably mixed.

1 Description and Distribution

Where does the robin fit into the scheme of things? Let us start with the most general category first. Our animal is a vertebrate (i.e., it has a backbone) and it is in the class Aves (i.e., it is a bird, one of about 8600 species in the world). There are two orders of birds: non-passerines and passerines. The passerines are the perching birds, a large proportion of which are songbirds. The passerine order is so numerous that it is divided into over fifty families, of which the family Muscicapidae (insectivorous, literally 'fly-catching', birds) contain about 1400 different species. Because the family Muscicapidae is so huge, it is in turn subdivided into nine or ten subfamilies. Our bird is in the subfamily Turdinae, which groups together all the thrush-like and chat-like birds.

Within the Turdinae there are over fifty genera, but it is here that the picture becomes less clearcut. Taxonomists – the scientists who specialize in classification – cannot agree on how large the genus *Erithacus*, which contains the robin, should be. According to many sources, the British bird sits in solitary splendour: it is the only species in its genus and bears the specific name *rubecula*: *Erithacus rubecula*. But some will add two other robins from the Far East, the Japanese robin and the Rukyu Islands robin. And if you go to the *Complete Checklist of Birds of the World* by Howard and Moore (1980), you will find that *Erithacus* has swollen to 25 species!

What we can say is that, of these twenty-four other species, whether in the same or in another genus, the closest relatives of the British robin that we are ever likely to see in Europe – if we are in the right place at the right time – are: the rufous bushchat, the thrush nightingale (or sprosser), the nightingale, the Siberian rubythroat, the bluethroat and the red-flanked bluetail. But, unless we are dedicated twitchers, we are only likely ever to see the nightingale and bluethroat in Britain.

Many birds which have the word 'robin' in their names are not true robins at all. For example, the popular cage bird, the Pekin robin, is in the babbler subfamily. Usually the word 'robin' is an epithet to tell us that the bird is robin-like in appearance or habits. The thirteen African robin-chats in the genus *Cossypha* (such

The nightingale reveals its close relationship to the robin in a number of ways. It is a bird that likes close cover. It has large eyes with which to penetrate the gloom, and which enable it to feed, as the robin does, in the early morning light and at dusk when other birds have given up. It has the same general upright stance and slightly long-legged appearance as the robin, but the two species part company when it comes to song. All the same, robins will sing at night (just as nightingales will sing during the day), so be sceptical when someone tells you that they heard a nightingale singing in Berkeley Square.

Another member of the plump, long-legged robin clan, a bearded scrub-robin, photographed by Mike near Victoria Falls when he was on safari in Zimbabwe. When Mike approached, it began to utter alarm calls, accompanied by a characteristic tail-flicking action, something which robins will sometimes do, especially when they are contemplating leaving a perch to fly off to another one.

splendid mouth-watering names the Victorian ornithologists gave them: white-bellied, chorister, black-tailed, white-browed, blue-shouldered, olive-flanked, snowy-headed, rufous-cheeked, grey-winged . . .) all have red or orange in their underparts. Similarly, there are the five African akalats, skulking robin-like forest-floor-dwellers, whose alternative name is 'whiskered redbreast', after their combination of flycatcher-like rictal bristles and the red on their breasts.

On the other hand, the three Asiatic/Malagasy magpie robins in the genus *Copsychus* were named 'magpie' to describe the male's black-and-white plumage, and 'robin' probably because of their aggressive behaviour and fighting qualities, which have resulted in their being widely trapped for the sport of cockfighting.

The 'robin' of New Zealand, *Petroica australis*, has the shape and stance of the British bird, and is renowned for its 'tameness and tendency to inspect the intruder'. It hasn't so much as a splash of red or orange anywhere, but it makes up for this with a splendid Maori name, 'Toutouwai'. Simpson and Day in their *Field Guide to the Birds of Australia* (1989) list five species of flycatcher-type birds called 'robins' in the genus *Petroica*. Their epithets − rose, pink, flame, scarlet, red-capped − confirm that they have shades of red in their plumage, although the deep rose-red breast of the rose robin is quite unlike anything you will find on a British robin! There are about another dozen Australian 'robins' in the other genera. Their vernacular names − hooded, dusky (also known as 'dozey'!), mangrove, white-breasted, eastern yellow, western yellow, pale yellow, white-faced, white-browed and grey-headed − indicate plumage or habitat features, but in this group it is more difficult to know what makes them 'robins', apart perhaps from their stance, for there is not a trace of red/orange anywhere in any of them. Then there are scrub-robins, bush-robins, blue robins, robin-flycatchers − the list goes on.

Quite often the name robin has been given by homesick emigrés to exotic birds which at least superficially resemble the familiar robin back in Britain. Perhaps the best-known 'non-robin robin' is the American robin, in fact a red-breasted blackbird-sized thrush which occasionally turns up in Europe, thereby living up to its specific name, *Turdus migratorius*, the migratory thrush. Former denizens of the British Raj had their own 'robin' to keep them company: the Indian robin, *Saxicoloides fulicata*, a perky little chat with chestnut underparts; while Brits in Jamaica fondly called the local tody − which isn't even a passerine, but more closely related to kingfishers − 'robin redbreast', simply on account of its bright red throat. Such is the appeal of the bird whose place in the affections of the British was finally confirmed when it was chosen in December 1960, after a lengthy correspondence in *The Times*, to be the official 'National Bird'.

There are a number of subspecies of the robin. The nominate race (the one first described) is the Scandinavian one, and therefore has the specific name repeated: *Erithacus rubecula rubecula*. The British

Perhaps the most famous 'non-robin robin' is the American robin, *Turdus migratorius*, a splendid, red-breasted, blackbird-sized thrush, which, as its scientific name suggests, is given to long-distance movements, occasionally to our shores. Photographed by Martin in the Rocky Mountains in Canada on return migration to its breeding grounds.

robin is the subspecies *E.r. melophilus*. The British robin breeds throughout the British Isles except for Shetland, though it is scarce in northern Scotland. The Continental form is widely distributed, being found almost throughout Europe and Asia Minor, extending as far east as the Caspian Sea and central Russia, with outposts in North Africa and the Azores. In the winter, there is a migration westwards and southwards of the Scandinavian and Asiatic birds into the milder parts of western Europe. The differences in appearance of the various races are quite subtle. Compared to, say, the *flava* wagtails (see any good field guide for pictures of *flava* subspecies, from our own yellow wagtail through to grey-headed, ashy-headed and black-headed), the robin does not vary spectacularly over its range. There is a general principle that birds tend to be larger in the cooler parts of the breeding range (Bergmann's Rule). The other common variation is in the general darkness or lightness of the plumage, which may be connected with such factors as rainfall (desert birds are paler) or isolation (birds tend to be duller where there are few competing species). See if you can make sense of the variations in these races of *Erithacus rubecula*:

Subspecific name	Geographical location
rubecula	W Europe, NW Morocco » NE Africa Grey-backed, light orange breast.
melophilus	British Isles Darker, more olive back, deeper orange breast (even darker in Ireland and Scotland).
superbus	Tenerife, Gran Canaria Very dark plumage, but intense ('superb') reddish-orange breast.
witherbyi	E Algeria, Tunisia Like our robin, but significantly smaller.
hyrcanus	E Turkey, S Russia » Iran, Iraq A darker race with a strong reddish tinge on the upper tail coverts
tataricus	W Siberia » Iran The palest of all the races of robin.

» = migrating to

In the British Isles, there are no races of the robin such as occur in, for instance, wrens. There is a St Kilda wren, for example, so why is there no St Kilda robin? The answer probably lies in the structure of the birds. The wren has short round wings not adapted for flying anything but short distances. Thus, island populations tend to become isolated and, over time, develop variations in size or plumage. Robins are better equipped for long-distance flight and thus avoid the isolation trap. The main difference between the British and the various Continental subspecies of the robin is not size or plumage, but behaviour. Compared to the friendly British fellow, with his penchant for perching on people's fingers and bed-posts, the Continental robin is a woodland skulker, clearly preferring not to be seen. Jake once lived in a flat in a small Swiss village. It had a balcony overlooking a stream and a bit of woodland. Winter-feeding on the balcony produced some interesting species, including redpoll, nuthatch and crested tit, but robins, although they could be heard in the vicinity, never came near. Even chopping up raisins or crumbling Cheshire cheese (not easy to find in a Swiss supermarket) would not have lured them out, for they are solitary and, in contrast to our robins, unfriendly.

By our standards, the Continental robin is not a friendly fellow, but everything is relative. For instance, the description of the *pit-roig* (the Catalan word for 'robin') in Joaquim Maluquer i Sostres' book, *Els Ocells de les Terres Catalanes*, could be about the British robin (except for the reference to Barcelona):

> El pit-roig és un dels moixons que més familiaritat mostren envers nostaltres, perquè es fa estimar per la confiança amb què se'ns acosta gairebé fins als peus . . . . Viu entremig de les bardisses dels jardins i dels parcs, fins i tot del centre de Barcelona.
> [The robin is one of the birds that shows most familiarity towards us, because it is known for the confidence with which it will approach us, even up to our feet. It lives in gardens and parks, even in the centre of Barcelona.]

Despite this Iberian evidence of robin-as-urban-dweller, the fact remains that the Continental robin is primarily a woodland bird,

People visit places like this in the Highlands of Scotland to see such specialities as capercaillie, crested tit and Scottish crossbill, but these old Caledonian pine forests with their understorey of juniper, blaeberry and heather are home to robins too.

much less in evidence than the British robin, which is everywhere and much in evidence. Well, almost everywhere. These robins breed throughout the British Isles except for Shetland, but they are scarcer in northern Scotland, probably because of the cold, wet climate (sorry, Scotland: we are looking at it from the birds' point of view), and because of the predominant heather habitat, which does not suit them either for feeding or for breeding. They occur, though, wherever you find tree-clad glens, as, for example, in the high Caledonian pine woods of the Abernethy Forest Reserve.

Elsewhere in Britain, the robin is so ubiquitous that one might start to think that it is the most abundant bird. So, how many robins are there really in the British Isles? It is undoubtedly one of the commonest resident breeding birds. According to the *Atlas of Breeding Birds in Britain and Ireland* (Sharrock, 1976), about 5 million pairs breed in Britain and Ireland, about the same as the estimated number for such everyday resident species as the blue tit and dunnock. Their numbers are exceeded by only a few species, such as the blackbird and chaffinch at 7 million and the wren at 10 million (except after severe winters). By contrast, the great tit weighs in at 3 million, the greenfinch at 1–2 million and the song thrush at 1 million.

What happens outside the breeding season? The corresponding *Atlas of Wintering Birds in Britain and Ireland* (Lack, P., 1986) suggests that over 10 million robins, about 15 per cent of the European total, are present in mid-winter. (It is assumed that the net movement in and out of Britain – see Chapter 8 – is small.) Again, comparison with other everyday resident species is interesting. Estimates for chaffinch and great tit are about the same, although the former's numbers may be swelled to as much as 20 million by arrivals from the Continent. For the same reason, blackbird numbers can be as high as 20 million, and song thrush 6–10 million. Greenfinch numbers are more modest, as we would expect, at 5–6 million. The figures for the blue tit at 15 million, dunnock at 20 million, and wren at anything from 12–20 million (depending on the severity of the weather) seem high, until we remember that the strategy of these species is to go for large clutch sizes in anticipation of a higher mortality rate during the winter.

Let us now have a closer look at the bird itself. It is surprising how difficult it can be to give an accurate description of even the commonest species. Though we may be able to recognise a male chaffinch, for example, how many of us could describe the distribution of colours in its plumage? Without consulting a field guide, try to write a description of a male chaffinch for someone who has never seen one before. Breast deep pinkish-brown, yes, but how far down the belly does it extend? Back: yes, dark. Dark green? Brown? Head: well, the crown is dark blue. Isn't it? White shoulder patch. Good. That's a good field character. But is there also a white wingbar? An old Shropshire name for the chaffinch is 'seven-coloured linnet' – but how are the colours distributed? You begin to understand the importance of accurate observation of a common species when you visit a part of the world which contains that species and also others which are very similar. No problems with, for example, the pied flycatcher in the British Isles, but what happens when you are in south-east Europe and have to separate it from the collared and semi-collared flycatcher?

Fortunately, the robin's plumage is easy to describe. Or is it? Without consulting your field guide, try to answer these questions:

1) How far does the orange-red of the breast extend: a) down; b) up?
2) There is some blue-grey plumage on a robin. Where is it?
3) Are there any wingbars on a robin?
4) Is the tail uniform in colour? Are there pale outer feathers, as in a chaffinch, for example?
5) What colour are the 'soft parts' (i.e., legs and bill)?

The two plumage features which are most often portrayed badly or not at all in popular drawings of the robin – most notoriously on Christmas cards – are: first, the extension of the red breast on to the forehead, i.e., above the beak; and, second, the delicate blue suffusion of feathering bordering the sides of the red breast.

As to wingbars, the tips of the greater coverts (the protective tract of feathers which covers the base of the secondary wing feathers) are buff in young birds and some older birds, and this produces a wingbar. As the tips wear, the wingbar eventually disappears. The tail, and indeed the rest of the plumage, is uniform.

The soft parts are the bill, legs and feet (the 'hard parts' being the feathers, which might seen paradoxical). The bird's insectivorous bill is horn-coloured, but can be dark to black. At its base are rictal bristles, which have the function of providing a sort of extension to the gape in order to catch insect prey, a feature extremely well developed in, for example, the nightjar. The robin's legs, which are a nondescript horn-to-brown colour, are noticeably long compared to, say, a dunnock's, and the effect is heightened by the splendidly upright chat-like stance of the robin, so reminiscent of its 'chatty' relatives, the stonechat, whinchat and wheatear.

When you think about it, though, the most striking feature of the robin (apart from its breast, of course) is that dark beady eye, which seems to be fixed directly, steadily, unflinchingly and sometimes uncomfortably on *you* even from a distance, from the fence at the bottom of the garden, say. The explanation for this dominant orb is partly that it really is a little larger than usual, which makes sense when you remember the robin's predilection for feeding in the first light of dawn and the twilight of dusk; and partly that it stands out quite starkly from the surrounding red plumage. But, whatever the explanation, you can never escape the sensation that the bird can not only see you, but that it is also studying you intently.

One observation we made was a direct consequence of our photographic interest in the bird. We discovered that robins use eyeshadow! Well, to be more precise, we noticed that, whenever a bird perches in a tree, it seems to position itself so that a shadow falls across its eye more often than can be accounted for by chance. This is presumably so that it can see better than if it had the sun shining into its eye, which in any case, being large, is more light-sensitive. Whatever the biological value to the bird, it was a source of great frustration to us when we realised how many of our pictures were marred by the presence of the bird's accursed 'eyeshadow'.

Experienced birdwatchers will agree with all that we have said in our description of the robin, but would add that you don't need any of that. In identifying any bird, you may use a combination of features: size, shape, colour, habitat, behaviour, flight, voice. In the case of the robin, its shape, even seen in silhouette, is enough to identify it: the combination of plump round body, long legs and upright stance gives it away every time. It really is remarkable how many stylized Christmas card robins are identifiably robins, even when the breast colour and other plumage features are hopelessly inaccurate. In fact, to draw a convincing robin, you can capture its essentials in four easy stages (see Fig. 1):

1) Plumpness and roundness: draw a circle.
2) Stance: add two long sticks for legs.
3) Pertness and alertness: add a big round blob for an eye.
4) Cheekiness: stick a little < on the front and a triangle for a tail.

And, hey presto, a robin!

Identification on silhouette alone is not confined to the robin, of course. Look at the outlines in Fig. 2 on page 22 for example and you should be able to identify the blackbird, lapwing, little owl, pheasant and robin.

It is thus an unmistakable bird, but occasionally aberrant forms are reported, most commonly albino or partial albino birds, which can cause a moment of excited belief that a rarity has arrived on your patch. But stay calm, because the robin-thing on the fence with

Fig 1.

21

Fig 2.

A robin's plumage seems straightforward, but how well can you describe it from memory? It is not easy to remember how far the orange-red of the breast extends, and many people are surprised to note that it actually extends above the eye and beak. The lovely delicate blue-grey suffusion bordering the red along the bird's flanks is also sometimes overlooked in illustrations. Ask people if the robin has a wingbar, and they might look puzzled. In fact, the tips of the greater coverts are buff in juveniles, forming a distinctive wingbar which disappears as the tips wear.

Insectivorous birds improve their chances of catching their moving prey by developing stiff bristles, called rictal bristles, at the base of the beak. You can see the robin's rictal bristles in the photograph, but there is no doubt that a picture of a nightjar's rictal bristles would be more spectacular. The bristles form a sort of extension to the gape, rather like the 'basket' that dragonflies make with their front legs, to scoop in anything tasty that passes by.

23

A robin 'wearing eyeshadow'! Just as we may shield our eyes with our hand to see better on a very sunny day, it seems that robins, when they perch, like to have a shadow across their eye, as shown in this picture. Our first reaction to our discovery that robins frequently perch so that their eye is in shadow was one of frustration, but we then realized that it was worth recording after all.

Now you see me, now you don't! It's a good idea to tame your garden robins to make them more accessible for photography, but sometimes, as in this case, you can become the victim of your own success. Mike, the bemused photographer in this picture, was on his own – no one else was present – so you might wonder how he managed to get this shot. All is revealed in Chapter 10.

From the sublime to the ridiculous, but these examples of robins on Christmas cards demonstrate how the 'robinness' of robins survives even the most extravagant artistic licence.

blotches of white on it really is just a robin, albeit a queer one. Albinism is not the presence of white so much as the absence of pigmentation. One might think of it thus: the plumage is colourless, like a sheet of white paper, waiting to be 'painted'. If the chemical signals are not sent to the feather bud, the emergent feather will remain white. Evidence from retrapping ringed birds in subsequent seasons suggests that the deficiency is persistent, so that the lack of pigmentation occurs in each new generation of feathers. Sometimes in the case of birds which are paler than normal (i.e., leucistic rather than albinistic), the deficiency rights itself. There is a record, for instance, of a wing-tagged red kite which started life as a pale individual, but which subsequently achieved normal plumage.

Albinism, the paleness or whiteness caused by lack of pigmentation, may give rise to completely white individuals, but partial albinism is more common. This individual, showing white on crown and wings and a marked paleness on the belly, proved very hard to photograph. We expended many days in fruitless pursuit as it dodged and disappeared behind every available piece of cover before it paused, and posed, just long enough for us to get this shot.

This partial albino was much more obliging, photographically speaking, as it was a hand-tame bird. Apart from the substantial white patch on the side of the neck, there were speckles of white on the throat and crown. Albinos, being more conspicuous, are regarded as having a correspondingly higher chance of being nobbled by predators, but this individual was a great survivor, having attended at the same garden feeding-station for three successive winters.

There is something really appealing about albino birds. You can be sure that any albino blackbird will excite public attention and usually merit a column and a photograph in the local newspaper. So, when we came upon a partial albino robin while we were trying to determine the boundaries of winter territories in the study area, we became very excited. And frustrated. The little beauty was constantly around people's feet while they were gardening, but it refused to come near the perches outside the hides which we painstakingly set up. When it finally disappeared in April, we heaved a sigh of relief! A consolation prize was offered to us, though, in the form of a robin with white feathers in breast and wings, which was eminently photographable because it came to a friend's house to be fed. She told us that this was the third winter that her 'white robin' had turned up, a confirmation that albinistic traits are persistent.

What happens to albinos? Or, to put it another way, why aren't there a lot more of them about? The theory is that they are more

vulnerable to predators because they are more conspicuous. So, albinos are less likely to survive and thus pass on their aberration to future generations. One summer, we trapped and ringed an almost completely white reed warbler in the reed beds in Christchurch Harbour, in Dorset, where reed warblers feed before taking off on their migratory marathon flight to Africa. It was seen – and enjoyed – by many observers over a period of 2 or 3 weeks before it finally disappeared. Of course, if we could see it so easily, perhaps predators could too.

If you keep birds in captivity, you can interfere with the natural processes and breed from birds with aberrant plumages. It is exactly the same technique which, say, rose-growers use to produce ever more exotic colour varieties of rose. What is the 'natural' colour of a rose? Presumably the pale pink of the hedgerow dogrose. Similarly with birds. It comes as a bit of a shock to discover, when you see your first flock of budgerigars in the wild, that they are little green birds. Whatever happened to the blue ones, the pink ones and the yellow ones? They are, of course, 'sports', aberrant forms that do not exist in, or at least do not survive in, the wild.

Aberrant robins have produced some wonderful false alarms.

Aberrant birds can produce heart-stopping moments. What would you make of this individual perched in a distant bush, for example? Given the habitat and its general appearance, we guessed that it was in the *Acrocephalus* genus to which sedge and reed warblers belong. That broad white crown stripe on a sedge-warbler type bird raised hopes of an aquatic warbler, but we quickly realized that that was ridiculous. It turned out, of course, to be a sedge warbler.

Reports in *British Birds* magazine show how easy it is to be fooled, especially when you are looking for rarities and are predisposed to be fooled, so to speak. The May 1979 and February 1980 issues of *British Birds* contained reports of aberrant individuals which resembled red-flanked bluetails. The May 1979 report described a robin seen on 17 October 1973 in a potato field on Cape Clear Island, County Cork, that must have caused missed heartbeats for the observers. They described it in their report as 'blue-grey above and white below, with a narrow orange gorget enclosing the white breast and throat'. Thirteen people watched this intriguing bird. Eight of them were happy that it was an aberrant robin, but the other five felt that:

> the possibility of other species, including Red-flanked Bluetail, *Tarsiger cyanurus*, had not been eliminated.

The bird was finally caught and examined in the hand, confirming that it was indeed a robin. But think of the flights of fancy and the racing pulses it provoked until that moment! Amazingly another bird of similar appearance was seen in the same area almost exactly 12 months later. Another oddity was recorded at Holme Bird Observatory, Norfolk, in September 1979. The observer says:

> It occurred to me that this bird might be an aberrant Robin, but I did not discount other species, including Red-flanked Bluetail.

He concludes (does one detect a note of regret?):

> It was only later, when reading [the account of the Cape Clear Robins] that I was left in no doubt that this bird was indeed an aberrant Robin with strikingly close similarities to those which occurred in Ireland in the Octobers of 1973 and 1974.

Can you tell the age and sex of a robin just by looking at its plumage? Once the juvenile robin has moulted out of its spotty brown plumage, it is virtually impossible to determine the age of a robin in the field. Moreover, there is — though we must assume that human and robins' eyes pick up quite different messages in this respect — nothing to choose between the plumage or size of male and female robins. Even in the hand there are few clues, at least outside the breeding season.

The ringers' *vade mecum* to the bird in the hand — Svensson's *Identification Guide to European Passerines* (1984) — is almost laconic:

> sex: male = female on plumage.

Not much help or comfort there. As to age, the best indicator is the colour of the *inside* of the upper mandible, hardly a field characteristic since robins, unlike, say, sedge warblers, do not usually position themselves in a low or open enough spot to give you much chance to see inside their mouths when they are singing or even yawning! The colour of the inside of the upper mandible and palate in young birds is – Svensson again – 'yellow to yellowish grey-white'. The palate may retain its yellow colouring in young birds through to the following spring, but the rest of the mandible progressively darkens to grey or grey-black. Other age indicators – at least in the hand – are the shape of the tail feathers, which tend to be pointed in first-year birds and more rounded in adult birds (a characteristic shared by many other passerines), and the buffish-yellow tips on most of the greater coverts in young birds, which soon wear away.

We thought we might have found another useful plumage character to separate the sexes in the field. We noted from observation of a number of pairs that the females seemed to be distinguishable in the field because they tended to be more rounded on the top of the head than males. This hypothesis was severely tested, however, because on several occasions when Mike thought that he had identified the female by this characteristic, the bird flew on to his hand for mealworms, something which only the male ever did!

During our study, we were able to separate the robins, at least during the breeding season, into males and females on the basis of their behaviour, usually the best indicator in species with apparently identical plumage. Even dunnocks, the ultimate nondescript mousy-brown birds, betray their sex and their intentions in Spring, when you can witness their brazen *ménage-à-trois* being enacted in the hedgerow bottom as the coquettish female flirts – for want of a better word – first with the one and then with the other.

In the breeding season, the male robin follows the female during nest-building and announces their territory by prolonged vigorous singing and the chasing off of intruders; during mating, the female is submissive and invites the male to mount. During the winter, when females hold their own territories and sing just as vigorously as the males, it is impossible to separate them except where changes of behaviour give clues.

Other aspects of a robin's everyday behaviour which excited our attention mostly had to do with plumage maintenance, particularly bathing and preening. People are often surprised at the way birds will plunge into icy water in the depths of winter and bathe. We regard

Care of plumage is, after food, the key to survival. The wing and tail feathers are the instruments of a bird's mobility, which it needs to catch prey and to avoid predators, and its body feathering is its guarantee of effective insulation against extremes of weather. Bathing is a vital element in plumage maintenance, especially in winter when birds are most vulnerable.

human beings who do the same thing off the beach in mid-winter as, to put it mildly, eccentric, and we are reluctant to believe them when they tell us how wonderfully bracing it is. (Although, to be fair, it must be so – like banging your head against a wall; wonderful once you have stopped.) But birds are doing it for a life-and-death reason: survival depends on keeping their feathering in perfect condition, which means: a) bathe; b) preen. The bathing, if you watch it closely, does not involve getting soaking wet, for that would serve to chill the body, with fatal results. Wetting the feathering is achieved by a succession of 'head-dipping' movements followed by a sort of showering over the back using the wings as propellers. The next stage is to get a good supply of oil from the preen gland, which is situated at the base of the tail, and then to apply it generously but meticulously to each feather, making sure that every barbule links every barb to produce an aerodynamically or hermetically efficient vane. One bird we observed spent about 5 minutes preening in this way, and we were struck by how rapidly it went about the business. Each application of preening oil to wing and belly feathers was followed by a complete shake of the wings and body to dislodge any surplus water. Presumably the bird preens *rapidly* so that it is less prone to chilling and less exposed to predators.

Preening generally follows bathing and is the occasion to re-oil the feathers and to comb them back into shape. If you want to get an idea of what is involved, pick up a dishevelled feather and try to restore it to its pristine condition. The bird gets the oil it needs for preening by rubbing its beak over the preen gland, which is situated at the base of the tail. The first picture (left) shows a female preening under her wing. The next two (right) show a male reaching the end of his preening sequence by scratching under his chin to sort out the much downier and softer body plumage. We are not sure why his beak is open but it certainly gives the impression that he is getting great satisfaction from having a good scratch.

Other avian strategies for plumage maintenance include such odd activities as anting and dustbathing. Starlings, for instance, are very fond of getting ants under their feathering, but we can be sure that the motivation is not so much one of masochistic pleasure (which presumably explains the wintry dips in the briny referred to earlier), as, we believe, a technique for dealing with feather lice and other parasites and generally keeping the feathers in trim. There seem to be two techniques if you wish to 'ant' yourself. The first and more indelicate method, which is quite hilarious to watch, is to plonk yourself down on some ants and let them crawl about under your feathering. The second and more sophisticated method is to pick up a live ant, hold it delicately in your beak and use it to preen your plumage, especially along the wing feathers. When you have forced your victim to deposit his formic acid (the ant family is known as the Formicidae from the Latin word '*formica*' for 'ant') on your plumage, pick up another one and repeat the process *ad libitum.*

Sunbathing by birds has all the look of an indulgence in a pleasurable activity, but the theory is that the ultraviolet rays in sunlight have a beneficial effect on the composition of the oils which cover the feathering, especially by the replacement of Vitamin D which is lost during preening. In this shot of a spreadeagled juvenile sunbathing at the base of a shrub, you can see the preen gland, which is normally concealed under its feathering.

Robins are not great 'anters', although we have a number of recorded instances. What they, along with other thrush species, love to do is to sunbathe. This favourite sunny-day activity, which is much easier to observe than anting, may have biological value. One theory is that the action of ultraviolet rays on the oils in the plumage helps to replace the Vitamin D in the feathering, which gets consumed during preening. Certainly the tendency is for the bird to spread itself in such a way that the preen gland is exposed. All the same, although it may be that it is light rather than heat which is

When birds indulge in activities which might expose them to danger, they tend to stay close to cover. Thus, favoured sunbathing spots (the same spot may be used at different times by different birds) are usually close to the base of a hedge or a shrub. In this case, the bird clearly decided that the base of our tripod was good enough: you can just see part of a tripod leg in the top left-hand corner of the picture. All very well for the bird, but it doesn't make photography any easier!

important to the bird (they tend to react to the sun even on cool, windy days), we can never shake off the impression that a bird spreadeagled on the lawn with the sun beating down is actually enjoying itself.

One hot summer's day, out to get our first action shots of robins sunbathing, we watched eagerly as a robin landed in front of us and spreadeagled its wings before settling down to a positively sensual spot of sun-worship. What a perfect shot it was – or would have been if the blessed bird had not chosen to situate its sunbed directly under the camera tripod! We were also determined to get photographs of robins engaged in another common avian activity: drinking. Think of those lovely shots of swallows dipping their beaks momentarily as they wing their way just above the surface of the water, or of finches taking a beakful and then swallowing by putting their heads back, looking for all the world as if they were gargling. Once again, the robin frustrated us. We rarely observed robins drinking at any of our regular waterholes. Why not? Don't they get thirsty? Part of the answer came one autumn morning, when we were at Sandringham in Norfolk, watching a mixed flock of siskins and crossbills. We had

At first glance this looks most unpromising as wildlife habitat. The fact that there are about 800,000 hectares of private gardens in the British Isles, an area which exceeds that of all RSPB reserves put together, means that private gardens have immense potential. We can be sure that the mature gardens, the ones planted up with trees and shrubs, will be prime territory for robins and other species. Let us hope that the rather barren gardens surrounding new housing will soon become havens for wildlife too.

gone there to 'twitch' a rarity, a two-barred crossbill. We noticed how frequently the siskins and crossbills came down to puddles to drink after struggling with a diet of dry larch-cone seeds. That was it! Robins must get such a lot of liquid from the food they eat that, unlike seedeaters, they have less need to come to water to drink, unless the weather is particularly hot, when they, like all creatures, will need to supplement their liquid intake.

Apart from some plumage variation, the biggest single difference between the British and Continental robins is, as we have seen, the former's close association with human habitation. Unlike its Continental counterpart, which tends to be a skulking woodland bird, our robin is equally at home in its original haunts of deciduous woodland and in parks and gardens, playing fields and allotments, as well as along field hedgerows and wood edges, and in copses and scrubby areas. It is catholic in its sylvan tastes, but seems to thrive in ancient managed woodland which has a mixed understorey of brambles and shrubs, interspersed with more open spaces, the sort of

Ancient coppiced woodland, a favourite breeding habitat for robins, and the route by which they began to be more closely associated with man and his activities. Bluebells (as well as certain lichens) are a characteristic of ancient woodland. The trees in this shot are mostly oak and beech or hazel.

places which are carpeted with bluebells in spring, a sure indicator of ancient woodland. It is no coincidence that the robin shares this favoured habitat with its close relative, the nightingale. Both species are primarily ground birds, and obviously feel at home in the protective cover provided by the understorey, where they can safely feed and rest and preen and nest. Unlike the nightingale, the robin is also beginning to colonize the Forestry Commission's gloomy conifer plantations, the sort of remote habitat much more favoured by its Continental cousin. And, as we have seen, at the other end of the scale, it has moved into all sorts of habitats associated with man. With this kind of range, it ought to be our commonest breeding bird!

Breeding density per square kilometre gives a clue to the bird's habitat preferences. According to the *Atlas of Breeding Birds in Britain and Ireland* (Sharrock, 1976), there were as few as ten breeding pairs per square kilometre in open Scots pine in Wester Ross, compared with 16–35 per square kilometre in hillside birch woods. Hedgerows with standards on farmland are also used when the robin population is high, the average density (according to the BTO's Common Birds Census) in the early 1970s being about 20 per square kilometre. But in good lowland woodland, the figure goes up to an average of 200–300 per square kilometre. Of course, the number of pairs will fluctuate anyway from year to year, influenced by many factors including the winter survival rate. Figures in the table below from the Royal Society for the Protection of Birds' Reserve at Minsmere (kindly supplied by Jeremy Sorensen), showing the number of breeding pairs each year, bear this out. The numbers in brackets are estimates.

1975 (25+)	1978 *c.*100	1981 *c.*80	1984 (90)	1987 *c.*192
1976 118	1979 *c.*40	1982 (*c.*45)	1985 (142)	1988 (*c.*100)
1977 *c.*120	1980 *c.*70	1983 *c.*50	1986 (152)	1989 225

Even allowing for census variations, the average figures for the numbers of breeding pairs show a remarkable fluctuation:

1975–79 81   1980–84 67   1985–89 162

2 Territory, Voice and Aggression

In the early part of this century, a remarkable man spent all his spare time watching birds. He used to get up before dawn every day and pursue his study of birds before setting off to work. Most evenings would find him out again. His name was Eliot Howard, a steelmaster by profession and for many years a director of the great steel company, Stewart and Lloyds, in the Midlands of Britain. In 1920, the fruits of his researches appeared in a book which has become a classic, *Territory in Bird Life*. In it he set forth his theory of territoriality, based on all those years of painstaking observation of the interaction of birds before, during and after the breeding season. Of course he was not the first to observe that animals are space owners. There are references throughout the ages to territoriality, starting with Aristotle, who writes in his *History of Animals*:

> In narrow circumscribed districts, where the food would be insufficient for more birds than two, ravens are only found in isolated pairs.

He also records that:

> a pair of eagles demands an extensive space for its maintenance, and consequently cannot allow other eagles to quarter themselves in close neighbourhood.

The Roman naturalist Pliny noted that pairs of eagles

> . . . need very considerable space to forage over . . . for which reason they mark out boundaries for their respective allotments.

Gilbert White, in his *Natural History and Antiquities of Selborne*, first published in 1789, put a slightly different complexion on things when describing male robins during the breeding season, whose rivalry is so intense

> . . . that they can scarcely bear to be together in the same hedge or field . . . and it is to this spirit of jealousy that I chiefly attribute the equal dispersion of birds in the spring over the face of the country.

Contemporaries of Howard in the United States of America,

studying humming birds, also theorized about the function of territoriality, as did the pioneer German ornithologist, J. F. Naumann (the one who lent his name to Naumann's thrush, one of the great British 'twitches' of 1989). Curiously, Eliot Howard seems not to have been aware of other people's work in the field, and independently set out his theories, which went beyond the proposition that territory was solely concerned with securing a food supply to include its value in acquiring and retaining a mate. He showed what he called the 'congenital foundation' of the intolerant and aggressive individual, supported by the evidence of aggressive territorial behaviour around the nest-sites of colonial nesting birds. Thanks to the painstaking fieldwork of Howard and other naturalists, most people are now aware that such endearing features of birds as their striking plumage or their sweet songs and calls have a proprietorial rather than an aesthetic value: being pretty is just as much about being a successful defender of your patch as about being attractive to your mate. While some questions remain unanswered, the theory of territoriality is now universally accepted. Indeed, what the writer Robert Ardrey called the 'territorial imperative' accounts for much of animal behaviour, including human behaviour, whether we like to admit to it or not.

We know now that the red breast and the distinctive song of the robin are weapons in its territorial armoury, and the bird gave us many opportunities to observe Eliot Howard's theories in action. In the garden in Ringwood, Hampshire, which constituted one of our main study areas, we had three feeding territories (see Fig. 3 on page 44), and this gave us good opportunities to observe competitive behaviour. In August, for example, there were frequent bouts of song competition, which seemed to go on for hours and hours, with the west garden bird singing and being replied to by the east garden bird. By the end of the month, the holding of territory had become almost like a ritual dance. To quote Mike's field notes for 24 August:

> East and West territories meet at the cotoneaster, front garden. East moved towards bush with occasional calls (a long 'twick'). West also moved towards the cotoneaster. East was in the buddleia. West postured briefly with head slightly raised and then flew at East. They rapidly flew in and around the buddleia then down on to the pavement and out of sight. East then flew across the road and West returned, taking up a position in the cotoneaster and giving a brief song in which there was surely an unmistakable note of triumph.

You see how hard it is not to become anthropomorphic when you are describing robins!

There seem to be a number of characteristics of a 'good' territory. It is not simply a matter of size, but of what is available within a given area. Sufficient feeding must be a prime consideration: a small insectivore and a carrion-eating vulture will need vastly different sizes of territory because of the difference in the abundance and availability of their prey items. A territory must also include, at least potentially, a suitable nest-site. Perhaps, though, in the case of many song birds, the most important requirement is a good song-perch from which to announce their territory. A colleague of ours

As the male moves round his territory, singing to announce his presence, he finds the top of a shrub, in this case a Portuguese laurel, does just as well as a tree. The perch is about 2.5 metres up. This may seem low, but we have seen robins occasionally sing from the ground.

One of the most important characteristics of a songbird's territory is a perch from which to sing. High perches give prominence, not least because you get a good bird's eye view, so to speak, over your territory. This male, in full song on his perch 3.5 metres up, was in fact cocking his eye at the female feeding on the ground below the tree.

observed, for example, disputes going on over a period of weeks, in which two blackbirds performed their ritualized battle in the same tree in her garden again and again. The explanation was soon clear enough: the tree, which was the best song-perch in the area, was on the border between their two territories; no wonder they could not settle the dispute! Territories have flexible borders. If an area can sustain, say, three territories and there are three holders available, then there will be three territories. If one holder disappears (and, given the mortality rate of small passerines, this is a frequent occurrence), either it will be replaced or, if not, the three territories will become two as the vacant one is encroached on by the surviving neighbours. Martin noted, for example, how three winter territories became two with the disappearance of one male (the one which hit the window and left that ghostlike outline shown in the photograph on page 101). Later a third male appeared and the size of the territories shrank again.

If Nature hasn't provided you with a song-perch, improvise. The same male completes his beating of the parish boundaries by taking advantage of a man-made artefact, in this case a telephone wire about 9 metres above the ground. Birds will sing from anything that is handy, whether natural or man-made, including television aerials, roof-tops and lamp posts. There are even records of robins singing while perched on a man's hand and being fed.

Other factors can influence the size of a territory, as for example the disappearance of one of the pair during the breeding season. In the case of one of the nests being studied, it was interesting that when the female lost her mate, she continued not only to feed the brood, but also to hold the territory, singing and driving off intruders, just as the male had done. But the size of the territory contracted because of the limited amount of time and energy she could expend on its defence.

To give an idea of the size and the boundaries of territory in relation to natural and man-made features, in the Ringwood garden in August, Mike mapped out the three territories of the robins (Fig. 3 on page 44). The garden contained the edges of three territories. One adult, West, had a territory bordering on to the south-west corner of the garden; another, East, bordered on the south-east corner of the garden, and the third was in the north (front) garden. The third soon disappeared, leaving the field open to the other two contestants.

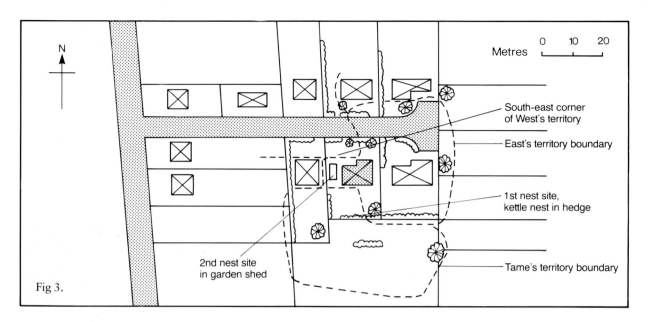

Fig 3.

South-east corner
of West's territory

East's territory boundary

1st nest site,
kettle nest in hedge

2nd nest site
in garden shed

Tame's territory boundary

Were East and West simply territorial rivals? Romance is hinted at in Mike's field notes:

By midwinter, West, who had now become tame, and East were visiting each other's territories. They were often in each other's company, yet still seemed confused. There would be occasional outbursts of aggression as one bird chased the other, and at other times they were content and completely tolerated each other. East would often raise its crest after flying at West. The tame bird, West, seemed to be singing more than East, so presumably is a male. Let us hope that the other is a female.

So what is the size of a robin's territory? Anyone seeking an answer to this question is drawn to the work of another great ornithologist, David Lack. In his immensely readable account of his studies of robins, *The Life of the Robin*, he describes how he mapped their breeding and winter territories. Howard had drawn the conclusion that territory size is fixed, but Lack was able to challenge this. As a rule of thumb, one can say that a robin's territory will be about half a hectare, but at Dartington, in Devon, where Lack carried out his mapping, he recorded territories varying in size from as little as 0.2 hectares to Texas-sized spreads of almost a hectare. The boundaries of territories will expand and contract somewhat as current owners disappear, or as pressure for space increases after a good breeding season and a mild winter, when more birds survive and are available to breed. Territory does not totally control breeding

Title: 'A Winter Woodland Scene'; pretty but barren, you might think. Woodland robins, however, will remain in their woodland haunts during the winter and hold territories, while other woodland species such as blue tits, great tits, coal tits and (if you are lucky) nuthatches and woodpeckers are happy to move into gardens to take advantage of your birdtable.

density, as Howard suggested. The average size of territories, as Lack noted in the case of robins and others have confirmed in the case of such species as the tawny owl and great tit, will shrink to accommodate more birds or expand to take up vacated space.

Simply stated, males and females each hold individual territories until pairing time, December in the south of England. But robins are not given to doing everything by the book, and one female of our acquaintance was positively perverse. During January and February,

45

we noticed a lot of activity in the garden, with this particular female chasing off males. She seemed to be saying: 'Not yet!' In fact, when it later seemed that she was going to pair up with a male, known as Tame, their relationship became increasingly stormy. She seemed unable to stop being aggressive towards him. The outcome was inevitable: Tame knew he was on a hiding to nothing, and went off to find himself another female who was living conveniently on the other side of the bungalow. Another female, Tame's new mate, using the kettle nest-site (see Fig. 3 on page 44), produced her own version of perverse aggressive behaviour. While she was building her nest, early in the season, she would go in while the male perched on a twig in the hedge above the nest-site. When she came out, she sometimes behaved as if she did not recognize him because she would go into a dramatic display, throwing her head back and puffing out her chest feathers. It lasted only a moment or two after which she presumably realized: 'Oh, silly me! That's my husband!' Occasionally the situation was reversed, as when he went in to inspect the nest and, on emerging, displayed momentarily at his mate who was on the twig perch. But it was always momentary and never violent. We assume that two hormonally-induced responses were in play, the territorial one not quite overtaken yet by the more powerful breeding one. It is interesting to note the influence of such external factors as weather on the holding and defence of territory. For example, if there is a male and a female on adjacent territories, mild weather at pairing time, i.e., in December, will act as a trigger to the pairing up process. They will move into each other's territory to act as a pair on a single territory. If it suddenly goes very cold again, they are likely to split up and go back to their own individual territories. At other times, the exact opposite is likely to occur, with robins as with other species; namely, survival during hard weather overrides all other priorities with little or no energy to spare for the expression of territorial rivalries.

The tendency to aggression in defence of territory is so strong that it can manifest itself very early in a robin's life. One morning in late August, for example, we observed a recently fledged bird with adult plumage only on its head and neck sitting on the fence and singing. It was confronted by a second singing bird, an adult, half a metre or so away. Within seconds, a third bird appeared, and all three were immediately involved in a fight. Despite its tender age, the juvenile gave a good account of itself before, wisely, retiring from the fray. Once a bird is in full territorial mode, his aggression can extend to other species at times, even though they cannot in biological terms pose any real threat. In February, Tame was so possessive of his territory that he not only drove off other robins which ventured into

The leafless boughs (left) betoken winter time, but this is in fact a male and female joining forces to set up a common territory. Yet it is not quite as simple as that, for this is the time of year when two urges conflict. On the one hand, male and female still have such strong territorial instincts that they display aggression to each other, while on the other, the stirring of the pairing instinct forces them to come together. The lower bird, with head thrown back to show as much of the red breast as possible, is the female in a momentary display of aggression towards her mate. He looks down somewhat bemused – is she mate or competitor? Of course he is just as likely to display aggressively at her, and this sort of conflicting behaviour will continue until the breeding season approaches and the appropriate hormones begin to dominate.

the garden, but was also frequently seen to attack dunnocks, which makes a kind of sense given their similar habitat preferences, and chaffinches, which does not. He also gave short shrift to house sparrows, perhaps with some justification, because house sparrows really are the thugs and bullies of the passerine world. We have seen house sparrows pull spotted flycatcher nestlings out of a nest-box and drop them on the ground, just because the nest was in their territory. We have also had several reports of similar treatment of swallow chicks. We noted during two breeding seasons what seemed to amount to sour grapes, when house sparrows, frustrated at not being able to use a blue tit nest-box (that 16mm makes all the difference!), constantly came to sit on the lid of the box and drive off the blue tits which had taken legitimate possesion of it. In both seasons, the 4–5-day-old young were found dead in the nest. The cause of death was almost certainly starvation following abandonment by their parents, who could no longer run the gauntlet of the bully-boy house sparrows. 'Who killed Cock Robin? "I" said the Sparrow, "with my bow and arrow."' This suggests that way back in

This picture, taken in April, shows a pair of robins on territory. They are the kettle pair: Tame, the male, and his new mate (whom he found after the previous female, who was very aggressive, had rejected him). Can you tell which is which? In fact, Tame is on the left; the fact that he is physically in a more dominant position is fortuitous. The female seems to be cowering slightly, but that may be because she was aware of the photographer's presence, and was not as used to him as Tame was.

48

Perched close to the base of a hedge, this male robin demonstrates the classic aggressive pose, head tilted back and throat and chest feathers puffed out to make the red colouring as prominent and threatening as possible. The picture was taken in January, by which time he had already attracted a mate. The task now was to repel all intruders.

the eighteenth century – this famous ballad was publised in 1744 – they knew about the nastiness of sparrows!

The famous ornithologist, Dr David Lack, in order to test his hypothesis that robins use their red breast only for aggressive purposes and not, as might be supposed, for display, did a series of experiments with stuffed birds. The sight of another redbreast in his territory, albeit a stuffed one, sent the local male robin into a rage, to the extent that he would even attack a piece of red cloth which in no way resembled a bird. We were fascinated by Lack's results and wanted to repeat the experiment for ourselves.

Frankly, we had a much more sordid motive. It was proving impossible to photograph robins exhibiting aggressive behaviour. Either the bird or the camera was in the wrong place, or, if both were in the right place, we blinked or coughed or otherwise missed our chances. In photography, it is quite legitimate to 'manipulate your subject', i.e., to create the conditions in which the subject is bound to do what you want it to and in the place where you want it to, a point which we develop in Chapter 10. So, eager for photographic immortality, we cajoled Paul Mason, an amateur taxidermist friend of ours, into letting us have a couple of robins from his collection, one of which he had mounted in an aggressive posture with throat puffed out convincingly. We set this one up in the territory of our local male in a prominent position atop a fence-post, one of his favourite perches. We polished our lenses, said a brief prayer to the Muse of Staged Photography, took our places behind the camera and waited.

The robin's reaction was stunning, baffling, outrageous: he totally ignored the stuffed intruder. Well, maybe he looked at it briefly but we could not be sure. The most definite reaction we could observe was that he seemed to go quiet for a while. What we were sure of was that he was not put out by the red breast being flaunted on his patch.

An aggressive territorial reaction can even be provoked by a 'rival' glimpsed in the wing mirror or the shiny hubcap of a car.

It was clear to us that he had not read Lack's book or he would have known how to behave. Or, more probably, he was not a 'normal' robin in that he was a tame bird and more secure in his territory than might otherwise have been the case.

Chance was, however, on our side. One January morning, while driving along a country lane in search of adventure, we came upon a robin singing on a roadside wire. He flew off when we got out, which gave us a chance to place our stuffed bird (which we carried everywhere at this time, just in case . . .) close to the hedgerow. The local robin returned to the wire about 10 minutes later and gave a loud burst of song. When he saw the stuffed bird, he flew into the hedgerow, gave a short burst of subsong, and then – God bless him! – flew towards the 'intruder' and displayed several times in textbook

David Lack confirmed that the function of the robin's red breast was not for use in courtship display but was a territorial signal to deter other robins. He demonstrated this by setting up stuffed robins in known territories and recording the behaviour of the occupier. Our attempts to reproduce Lack's experiments were successful, as this picture shows. Robins in territorial fighting tend to attack each other about the head, and especially the eyes. This outraged attacker perched practically on his victim's head and proceeded to peck violently at it.

manner, breast and throat puffed out magnificently. He was joined later by a female and it seemed that the two of them were a little confused, as they started to display at each other with the intruder taking a spectator role, as it were. The female did at one point give a sky-pointing display at the intruder before the two flew off.

Another experiment 2 days later was more spectacular. A different pair of birds was quickly attracted by the stuffed bird which we had placed within their territory. The male behaved much as the previous one had done: songburst, short display and departure. But the female was obviously made of sterner stuff. After eyeing the intruder malevolently for a few seconds, she virtually began to dive-bomb it, pecking at it violently before retiring after each attack to her perch to swear under her breath. Twice she even managed to come away with a beakful of feathers. We ran out of film before she ran out of puff. We remained to observe, though, watching her feeding some distance away. She was working her way along the hedgerow towards the stuffed bird, which was looking a bit ragged by now. When she was about 7 metres away, she noticed it and immediately launched a fresh attack before moving on. The violence of her attack reminded us of university lecturer David Harper's observations at Cranborne, where he confirmed that robins will sometimes fight to the death in defence of territory, inflicting terrible injuries on each other, particularly to the head and eyes. Not all sweetness and light, after all, our little bird.

Another incident with the stuffed robin, which by this time had become a little the worse for wear, occurred at a feeding station in a friend's garden in Fordingbridge, Hampshire. The table was being visited by a variety of species, including nuthatches. We happened to have a few mealworms in our pocket, so to speak, and had a robin coming to the table in no time. Hoping for better shots of 'robin-attacking-stuffed-intruder', we set up our stuffed bird on the table. The Fordingbridge robin gave it two or three bursts of song, but did not attack it. The nuthatch, however, which had long dominated the food supply on this table, was astonished that the stuffed bird did not fly off at his approach, and had no hesitation in dive-bombing it mercilessly!

Voice is perhaps the most powerful announcer and defender of territories. A range of songs and calls establishes rights, warns off trespassers, and effects communication to kin within the territory. Describing bird song and calls in words is notoriously difficult: one man's 'pee pee pee' is another man's 'tiu tiu tiu'. Even calls which are relatively easy to describe, such as those of the spotted flycatcher in the following table, produce some

A robin on territory is incensed by the sight of the red breast of a rival, to the extent that it will attack a stuffed bird or even a piece of red rag. Sometimes, a greater threat will outweigh this reaction, as in the case of a garden feeding-station where nuthatches had become so proprietorial that they were able to drive off other birds. The local robin therefore did not venture near the stuffed robin which we had placed on this post, despite the copious supply of mealworms which we had strewn below to tempt it. The nuthatches tried to drive off the stuffed intruder, but when it inexplicably (from their point of view) failed to flee, one of them attacked it violently.

interesting variations when attempts are made to render them phonetically:

A Field Guide to the Birds of Britain and Europe   A very thin grating 'tzee' and a rapid 'tzee-tuc-tuc' (or, in the Spanish edition, 'un agudo y rascante "tche" y un rápido "tche, tec-tec"'!).

New Generation Guide to the Birds of Britain and Europe   A thin 'tsee', sometimes followed by a quiet 'chuck'.

Hollom Popular Handbook   Call is a thin 'tzee', much like a robin's but shriller and more scratchy. Alarm is 'tzeec-tzucc'.

Reader's Digest Book of British Birds   Its usual call is a shrill, robin-like 'tzee'; and the alarm note 'whee-tucc-tucc' recalls that of the stonechat.

Distinguishing between 'tzee', 'tsee' and 'whee', or 'tuc', 'tucc', 'tzucc' and 'chuck' is not easy. Our favourite description, though, comes from the *Hamlyn Guide to Birds of Britain and Europe*, (Bruun & Singer, 1978) which sums it all up with the judgement: 'Call is a sharp "zit" '.

In his book about bird photography, *Birds Wild and Free*, A. W. P. Robertson states his conviction that transcribing bird sounds is a thankless task:

> The raven's croak, for instance, has been rendered as 'pruk', 'glog' or 'whow', but one has only to imagine oneself setting out to find a bird that said 'glog' to be transported straight into the world of Lewis Carroll and the slithy toves.

So, when describing the robin's calls and songs, rather than compound the error, we shall quote, in full, from that impeccable authority, Witherby's *Handbook of British Birds*, Volume II:

> The British Robin
>
> Voice: Commonest note scolding 'tic tic', repeated rapidly when excited and much used at roosting time.
>
> Call a high-pitched thin 'tswee' much like Spotted Flycatcher, also a soft thin 'tsit' or 'tsip' with variants 'tsip-ip' or 'tsissip'.
>
> A note of anger is an explosive hiss like spit of cat.
>
> Note of nestlings and of female when being fed by male is peculiar tremulous sound impossible to render satisfactorily, something like 'sweez-eez-eez-eez'.
>
> Song: Melodious and varied, though impressing many observers with a certain melancholy quality, is delivered in short liquid warbly phrases, some rather shrill, of commonly about 1–3 seconds' duration with pauses between; sometimes imitative.

One thing is for sure: the robin's song is one of the most familiar and easily recognisable in our gardens, hedgerows and woodlands. Different people, not necessarily dedicated birdwatchers, have described it to us variously as 'vigorous', sometimes as 'wistful', sometimes as 'sad', and, nine times out of ten, as 'sweet'. In our view, the robin's song has a falling cadence which we would liken to that of the willow warbler. It varies in intensity with the time of year, being particularly vigorous in Spring, and more subdued in Autumn, the time when we are prone to hear undertones of 'sadness' and 'wistfulness' in reflection of our own mood about the approach of the dark and barren season.

It is interesting to note that the robin is one of the few British birds that sings regularly in the Autumn. The species is also unusual in that females as well as males hold territories outside the breeding season

Robins singing near street lamps at night probably account for all those reports of urban nightingales in full throat (and definitely so for those reported in January, when this picture was taken!). The light from the street lamp simulates daylight, or at least dawn, thus encouraging territorial song from the indefatigable robin.

and therefore females also sing territorially. Indeed there is some evidence that female song is more usual than male song in Autumn. Song from female birds is exceptional in British and European birds, although the female wren has a sort of 'whisper song' and it is known that female dippers sing. Other exceptions are those species where the female takes the initiative in courtship, such as the red-necked phalarope. Outside Europe, there are instances of female song, including the bizarre behaviour of the female yellow-billed sparrow (a Central American species, *Arremon aurantiirostris*), which actually sings while incubating. But the most spectacular examples of female song occur in the so-called 'duetting' of some tropical species, including some African barbets and African shrikes. This is either unison or a kind of antiphonal singing between male and female, in which the timing is so incredibly accurate that you could be forgiven for thinking that all the singing was coming from one bird. Significantly, it is very rarely the female that initiates the interchange. In any case, duetting is to do with maintaining the pair bond, not holding territory, so our female robin and her Autumn singing have some claim to uniqueness after all.

The song may be given from low in the hedge or from an outer twig of a tall tree, but as often as not, you cannot actually see the bird, which adds to the magic and mystery. It is at its most magical and mysterious, we think, when you hear it at night. No, it is not a nightingale, even if you are in Berkeley Square, but a robin. One cold January morning, Mike was bravely out at 6am. Shortly after that, he noted a robin was singing by the street lamp. It was 6.20am, and still pitch dark. He heard it again at 5.50pm in the evening. It was dark again. The bird was still singing 20 minutes later when our hero, frozen to the marrow, crept back home to thaw out and write up his field notes.

The robin's calls, listed and described in the *Handbook of British Birds* quoted earlier, are mostly used to communicate on territory with its kin: feeding calls, contact calls, warning calls and, when its territory is invaded, that hissing explosion of anger 'like spit of cat'.

One of its commonest calls, however, may have another function. It seems to use its drawn-out 'tsit' or 'tsip-ip' call (which Mike swears is 'twick'; see what we mean?) as it approaches the limits of its territory, and this could be an exploratory sound to test where the edge is, as if it were saying: 'Is anyone there?'

The soft phrases, which are called subsong, are used exclusively to communicate with kin. In April, we noted that during feeding times at the nest there were often quiet calls from both adults, but especially from the male. When the male arrived to feed, he would sometimes give a short burst of subsong from a perch near the nest.

3 Courtship to Nest-building

One of the most spectacular sights in the animal kingdom is display courtship, where males use various combinations of colour, sound and gesture to attract females. Robins are disappointing in this respect. The red breast, as we have seen, is used for threat displays to hold a territory against rivals and not for courtship display. No, the cock robin has a basic strategy which is pragmatic in the extreme: he simply sets up a territory and waits for a female to choose him! In many species, once the male has been successful in securing a mate, the pair will later indulge in a further type of display where they perform a variety of dances and posturings that are sometimes positively balletic. Here again, robins are functional about the whole process: no display, no billing and cooing, no foreplay, just straight to business. Well, almost no foreplay. Mating is achieved by the rather inelegant, to our eyes, 'treading' technique and is usually stimulated either by the male pecking or by the female lowering her head and slightly humping her body. But Mike recorded some fine detail to demonstrate that sometimes attendant features can be quite appealing:

> The kettle pair were observed mating in a lilac tree. The male tried to mount the female but surrounding twigs prevented it. The female then moved her position, leaned forward into a horizontal stance and quivered her wings. The male then mounted her. This was then immediately repeated a further two times. During the mating, the male was constantly wing flapping to retain his balance.

There is something very beautiful in that image of trembling wings. Martin had his day too and showed that, if there is not much foreplay, there is something suspiciously like afterglow. The matter-of-fact tone of the following entry in his field notes cannot conceal the atmosphere of a sort of time-suspended post-coital state, as if the birds were in some sort of ecstatic trance:

> Pair of robins seen feeding, later seen mating. Male then flew a short distance away to the right of the spot where mating took

place, while the female flew to the left. Both remained motionless for about 20 minutes before carrying on feeding again.

Coition amongst robins takes place in the period of nest-building and egg-laying, but ceases thereafter. It may occur several times each day. For example, in the case of the robins that were coming to the mealworms, we recorded, to quote the field notes: '11.30am. Pair mated five or six times between mouthfuls.' Later in the day, ardour had subsided: '1.30pm. Female in birch, male tried to mount, female brushed him off.'

Having been a little brusque about the robins' lack of finesse during initial courtship and mating, let us now redress the balance. One of the most beautiful aspects of pair-bonding that you will ever observe is courtship-feeding, which seems to become more important after nesting has started. One of our correspondents captured the essence of it:

something we had never seen before . . . the female asking the male for food, just like the babies do. [Joan Webster, Burley, Hampshire]

This picture shows the act of mating which is so brief and unpredictable that you are lucky to see it, let alone capture it on film. In this case, the birds had already mated once an hour before, so we were alerted when the female uttered a soft subsong to attract the male's attention. He flew down to her, she lowered herself in the characteristic invitation pose and he mounted her. It was over so quickly that this was the only shot we could take.

Courtship-feeding is a powerful way of maintaining the pair bond throughout the breeding cycle. Here a begging female is shown calling and wing-quivering to the approaching male, who is carrying a gift of food to her.

The female's courtship-begging for food does indeed involve opening of the beak, but it is the wing-quivering that makes her so irresistible – at least to our eyes. It seems to symbolize her dependence and vulnerability during the time of breeding, a time of great physical stress for her. She is so completely different in posture and behaviour now from the Amazon who was defending her territory a few weeks earlier with just as much machismo as any male. To heighten the delicious tension, we noticed that she often preceded her display with a courtship-begging call, a lovely tremulous sound something like 'sweez-eez-eez-eez', which she uttered as she went round the territory to coax her mate to feed her. Sometimes, when the male had food in his beak and the female was nowhere to be seen, he would give a softer version of the same call, as if to say: 'I've got food for you. Do you want to be fed?' On several occasions the male, having taken a mealworm from the hand, would give that call before flying off to feed the mealworm to the female. Most of the courtship-feeding we observed took place early in the morning. We noted too that it was often an accompaniment to other activities. For example, whenever the female took building material to the nest, the male usually visited

the nest-site and fed her there, assuming of course that he had located a suitable food supply on which to draw. This served only to increase the drama and delicacy of performance.

In any animal study, there is a danger of being anthropomorphic, attributing human motives and feelings to the creature, and we have no doubt fallen into this trap. When it comes to courtship-feeding,

Against a backdrop of plum blossom, the beautiful act of courtship-feeding unfolds. The male will often return three or four times with food before the female ceases her importunate calling and wing quivering.

60

we say unashamedly that what we witnessed were touching displays of tenderness of the male for his mate. Yes, we know that courtship-feeding is a part of pair-bonding, that it has a simply-explained biological function and value, that there is, to use the unlovely jargon of our modern world, a 'pay-off'. We also know that it is beautiful to see, and we make no apology for being sentimental about it.

Pair, court, mate. And select your nest-site. Our knowledgeable Victorian egg-collector, the Reverend Atkinson, paints a wonderful word picture of the robin's nest and its sites:

> A hundred different places, too, the little bird selects for the site of its nest; often being such, moreover, as to illustrate their confiding fearlessness, as much as the result in them of the pressure of winter cold and hunger. In the tilt of a wagon; in a steam-boat; in a room of the cottage; near a blacksmith's forge; in the constantly-used garden-shed, as well as in the ivy or evergreen bush; or on the bank, or in the hedge; or in a hole in the old ruin or bank or house-wall; all places seem to suit it alike.

In fact, most nests are located on or near the ground in the vegetation of an earthbank or hedge (e.g., 211 out of 315 sites found and described by Arthur Whitaker, an indefatigable nest-finder, who in his lifetime meticulously recorded the details of over 21,000 birds' nests). It is probable that the proportion of nests in walls and buildings is greater in the south and east of England away from the deep lanes and sloping woods of the west and north. And these are the ones we are more likely to find, since they are by definition closely associated with human activity.

During our study, we found nests in nest-boxes (including the ill-fated nest in a kettle, the saga of which is told at the end of this chapter); sheds (one in an orchard shed, on top of a pile of empty fertilizer bags, which carried dire warnings about the hazards to health of inhaling the dust from them; and another one in a tin marked 'Rat Poison'); garages (one where the bird used a pigeon hole which had been stuffed with rubbish; another where the robin nested on top of an old altimeter from an aeroplane next to a timeclock); in workshops (one nest in a cardboard box, on which some wag wrote a works code 'R.O.B.1N'); in inaccessible parts of farm machinery (there are several accounts of nests in tractors, whereby the occupants found themselves taking short trips into the surrounding countryside without leaving the nest!); in hanging baskets, including one containing cacti. The incredible thing about this last site was that after the first brood had gone, the old basket was removed and

Robins are well-known, if not notorious, for their choice of nest-sites. This pair took a fancy to a compartment of a shelving rack in a garage. The altimeter is an integral part of the nest, obviously providing a stable frontage to support it, and we discount the theory that the bird wanted to know how far above the ground she was (1.5 metres in fact).

Spotted flycatchers and robins seem to like hanging baskets as nest sites even when the baskets are located near a door which is in frequent use. Sometimes the house-owners do not discover that their hanging basket is occupied until they hear the chirping from 1-week-old chicks, despite the fact that they may have watered it twice daily. This robin's nest was successful, bringing off a brood of at least four young.

Tame and his mate tried unsuccessfully to nest in a kettle placed in a hedgerow. Many nests in these situations, however, do produce young, just as this one did. It is best if the kettle is fairly well hidden. In this photograph, some strands of vegetation were temporarily tied back to obtain a clearer view.

Another unusual site, this time in the store of a big workshop. The storeman, anxious that they should not be disturbed, labelled the box in which they had built their nest. Out of habit, he gave the box a Part Number: 'R.O.B.1N'.

replaced with a different one, in which the robins promptly built a second nest and raised another successful brood.

They will also make use of the nests of other species, such as the roomy cup of an old song thrush nest or the cosy holes left behind by green or great-spotted woodpeckers. There are even cases where robins have used occupied nests of other species, by ousting the resident bird – nightingale and redstart have both suffered this indignity. Very occasionally, robins will literally move in and share the nest, as for example in the case of a pied wagtail who happily continued to sit on her clutch side by side with a robin who happily sat on hers. Both broods were successful. There are records of sites which are even more bizarre, including some that are absolutely macabre. One record is of a nest stuffed, believe it or not, in the body of a dead cat. Another, quoted in Chris Mead's book, *Robins*, is of a robin which built a nest in the skull of a hanged thief; the nest was only discovered when they took the body down from the gibbet!

The nest itself is a bulky untidy mass of dead leaves, grass and moss, quite nicely lined (but not as prettily as that of, say, the small

A nest in an open-fronted nest-box, ideal for robins. Nothing unusual about that, you might think. But look a little more closely. The clutch of eggs appears to be in a depression on the rim of the nest. In fact there was a clutch of five, of which three were on the rim, as shown in the picture, and two were in the main cup. We know that the female actually laid them in this way, but we have no idea why, or why the birds subsequently deserted the nest.

finches, like the linnet or goldfinch, or even of the dunnock) with fine roots and hair but rarely with feathers. When it is in a cavity, such as a nest-box or hole in a wall, it can give the impression of being 'roofed' in the manner of a house sparrow's nest. But to see what the nest is like, you first have to find it! To quote Brigadier Clive Simson, another seasoned nest-searcher and the author of *A Bird Overhead*: '[The robin is] just about the most secretive and cunning of our birds.' Finding nests when the birds are on the eggs is very difficult. If you are looking for nests when the birds are building, you have a better chance because they can go quite openly to the nest-sites at times. The problem here is that, if the birds see the nest being examined at the building stage, or when the clutch is incomplete, they are very likely to desert unless they are well used to human beings. Once they are feeding young, however, they are no more difficult than any other bird. The female will leave the nest to be fed by the male, and will utter a begging 'wheeze' as well as a characteristic 'zit' call. Providing she has not become aware that she is being observed, she will return at once – and alone – to the nest after feeding.

Robins are usually circumspect, however, as they approach the nest, so you sometimes do not know where the nest is until they fly away again with, for example, a faecal sac. They have, too, a wonderful habit of 'false visiting', calculated to drive the nest-searcher crazy and finally to convince him or her to take up a less frustrating pastime like beetle identification or unravelling string. So, when you see a robin leave a place 'furtively', pausing to eye you 'suspiciously', by all means check the site out, but do not be disappointed if you find nothing. He may have been 'kidding'; worse still, while you are in the hedge bottom tearing yourself and your clothing to pieces, he is probably visiting the true nest-site!

In the case of your own garden birds, here is a useful tip if you want to locate your robins' nests. During the winter, it is possible to see male robins prospecting for nest-sites: a bird will go back to the same spot again and again, and it is a fair bet that he is talking himself into a site for a nest in the spring. This was so in the case of the kettle robin, which constantly visited the kettle during the winter, and would sometimes go into it as many as four or five times in one day, staying in there for quite a long time almost as if he were 'trying it out for size'. He may also, of course, have been using it as a roost site.

Once the nest-site is accepted by the female, she will start gathering materials. We reckoned we could improve our chances of filming a

female in the process of gathering nesting material if we made a supply of stuff more easily available to her. To this end, Martin went around the hedge bottom gathering leaves, which he piled in what he hoped would be an attractive heap conveniently close to the nest-site. She ignored them, of course, probably because they were slightly damp, and continued to forage further afield.

The timing of nest-building is undoubtedly influenced by the prevailing weather conditions. In his notes, Mike, while observing the birds at the kettle nest-site in late February states:

> 16th: A warm day. The female spent the day building her nest in the kettle. Only two or three short spells of building observed. On two occasions the male flew into the hedge while the female was present as if on an official inspection visit. Mostly dried leaves are used.

'Robin sporting handlebar moustache'? Female gathering nest material, actually. The base of the nest is usually made from coarse materials, especially dead leaves.

While bringing back nest material, this bird suddenly became aware of the the photographer's presence. Before flying to the nest, it made a couple of false starts during which it briefly adopted this pose. Robins will often bob into this tail-up posture and utter their ticking alarm note in reaction to a cat or to some other potential hazard in the vicinity of the nest.

17th: Much cooler. Female seen leaving the nest with nesting material, having entered without any. Why? Speculation: the urge to get on with nest-building is conflicting with a prior instinct to clean and prepare the site for a new nest. At this stage nest is half-built, i.e., with a good foundation to about half the depth of the kettle.

19th: Still much cooler. Site checked. All nest-building activity ceased. Kettle virtually empty. Both birds seem to be avoiding the area.

On that day, Mike noted that the ground beneath the kettle was strewn with the leaves and moss which the female had so painstakingly carried to the nest a few days earlier. The kettle was reoccupied by the same pair later in the season and a complete nest built, but it was unfortunately predated by a cat.

4   From Egg to Fledgeling

As soon as the nest is complete, the female is ready to lay her brood of four to six eggs at the rate of one a day, usually early in the morning. One March morning, Mike was up at 6am to set up for photography. He noticed that the male was around and singing, but the female, normally very much in evidence, was nowhere to be seen. Finally, at about 6.40am, she appeared from the nest and the male soon flew down from his song-post and fed her. Mike checked the nest and found that the first egg had been laid. Once the female has a complete clutch, she will then start the process of brooding the eggs, a process which takes about a fortnight. This is achieved by the transfer of her body heat to the eggs, for which purpose she develops a naked 'brood patch', created by the loss from her belly of the feathering which normally acts as an insulator and would otherwise prevent the heat from getting to the eggs. In some passerine species, such as the sand martin and blackcap, both parents will brood. Although even in these cases the female does the lion's share (or should it be the lioness's share?), the males can develop something of a brood patch, too. The male robin, however, stays aloof, regarding his function as one of protecting the territory, warning off predators, and feeding the female to reinforce the bond between them.

The eggs themselves are, in our view, pretty, but for a more objective view, we quote a scientific description, taken from *A Field Guide to the Nests, Eggs and Nestlings of British and European Birds* (Harrison, 1975):

> Subelliptical. Smooth and non-glossy. White or very slightly tinged blue: speckled, spotted, freckled, faintly mottled or finely blotched with shades of buff to light brown, and sometimes light purple or purplish-buff. Markings very sparse to profuse; at times fine and obscuring ground colour. Often cap or wreath of more concentrated marks at larger end. Rarely, confined to this; or unmarked. 19.9 × 15.4mm.

The Reverend Atkinson, our unrepentant oologist ('oologist' is the grown-up version of the little boy 'egg-collector'; the term is designed to give respectability to a disreputable practice), is more succinct:

The photograph on page 62 showed a nest in a hanging basket. Once the young had fledged, the house-owners took down the basket and replaced it with another one which was, as this photograph shows, immediately occupied by the same pair. They produced a clutch of five eggs, which all hatched and eventually yielded five healthy fledgelings.

The shell is white, more or less freckled with light red.

He adds:

How beautiful the Robin's eggs are when just laid; and how they lose their peculiar pinky loveliness from being blown.*

While the female is brooding the clutch, the male frequently feeds her, taking her any reasonably-sized prey items. When the young first

---

* Egg-collectors pierce each end of the egg in order to expel the contents by blowing through one of the holes. We use the present tense 'pierce' rather than the past tense 'pierced' because, unbelievable as it may seem, there are still egg-collectors in Britain today, mostly old men who refuse to grow up, and who employ unprincipled young men to go and get the eggs for them. Naturally, the most prized eggs are those of rare birds, so the eggers are rarely content with anything less than the full clutch, nest included. Egg-collecting is, of course, illegal as well as immoral, and we should all be vigilant and report any suspicious activity to the RSPB.

hatch and are very small, the male starts bringing in items of food for them. In the BBC's wildlife film, *Who Really Killed Cock Robin?*, made about David Harper's Cranborne study, there is a sequence showing the male parent, whose unsuccessful struggle to stuff a huge prey item down the gullet of a nestling was matched only by the latter's equally unsuccessful struggle to swallow it. It seems likely that this was an example of an inexperienced male. We recorded a similar instance, when the male returned to the nest with a caterpillar about the size of the Loch Ness Monster for his young, which were in fact about 5 days old then. He held the beastie by its middle and tried to push it down the gape of one of the chicks. The caterpillar, of course, bent double and was too fat to swallow, despite considerable valiant gulping efforts by the chick. After a time, the adult removed the caterpillar and re-presented it to the same chick and the same thing happened again. After watching the chick for a while, the adult presumably realized that things were not going according to plan, so he repossessed the caterpillar a second time. This time, though, he had hold of one end of it. At this particular moment, another chick started begging quite vigorously (as only babies can), received the caterpillar end on and swallowed it as deftly as if it were a Whitstable oyster.

Our own observations suggest that it is more usual for the male to

Male passing small item of food to female at nest. The fact that the female has raised her body and is in effect standing is an indication that there are young in the nest. Actually this photograph was taken on the day when the eggs hatched.

A caterpillar is just protein-in-a-bag if you are a hungry robin chick. There can be problems if the parent holds the caterpillar by the middle, causing it to double up and become the equivalent of a doorstep sandwich, good to look at but difficult to get into the mouth.

Caterpillars and other larvae are the prime food items for robins during the Spring and Summer. In this case, the adult has brought in a worm for its chicks. Robins are most likely to locate worms early on damp mornings when the worms are near or on the surface.

bring in small food items in the early stages. In any case, if the female is there, he does not feed the young directly, but always passes the items to her, so that she can feed them. As the chicks get bigger, they can cope with larger food items, and both parents will pop juicy morsels down hungry throats. Their diet is not one of which a vegetarian would approve. Most of the protein comes in the form of insects (moths, flies, etc.) and especially insect larvae, but they may also get the odd ant, spider or centipede. A special 'Sunday joint' sort of treat takes the form of a nice (if you are a bird) juicy earthworm. Robins, although basically insectivorous as their bill testifies, also feed on vegetable matter, such as weed seeds, some grain, and fruit and berries, but the fact remains that the young in the nest have a primarily meat diet.

The time when the young are in the nest is the busiest in the life cycle of the parent birds, as there is much to do apart from feeding the young. The chicks are vulnerable and need to be protected from

Nest hygiene is important to keep parasites, predators and disease at bay. It starts in earnest with the removal of the pieces of eggshell on hatching day. Normally adults remove the eggshells by flying off with them, but this female surprised us by swallowing at least some of the pieces, behaviour not previously recorded in robins as far as we know.

excessive heat and cold, from predators and even from disease and parasites, which is why hygiene is so important. House-cleaning starts at once with the removal of eggshells, usually by the expedient of picking them up in the beak and flying off with them. In one case, we observed something unexpected. On the day that the young hatched, the female frequently stood up, looking at the young and also pecked lightly at the nest contents. This happened each time the male arrived with food. On one occasion, she pecked at the nest and came up with a large piece of eggshell in her beak. This we photographed immediately, fearing that she would fly off with it (we had earlier seen one of the parents in the front garden with something large in its beak which we had taken to be an eggshell), but instead, to our astonishment, she actually ate it. We later saw her swallow a smaller piece of shell. Curious now to see if this behaviour would be repeated – and to get more shots of it (having run out of film at the critical moment earlier in the day) – we took two eggs from a nest

As every parent knows, a baby is a simple machine with an input and an output. The output of nestlings is a faecal sac in which the unwanted matter is neatly packaged in a gelatinous casing. The picture shows how the chick positions itself, rear end up, so that the parent robin can remove the faecal sac.

Both parents waiting to feed the young in the hanging basket. You can tell that the photographer is nearby, because both adults have mealworms in their beaks.

which had been predated, broke the shells in half, serrating the edges with scissors to make it look as if they were half shells from a hatching, washed them thoroughly and placed them in the occupied nest while the female was away, so that when she came back to the nest she would find pieces of eggshell there. The male arrived with food and then flew off with one of the shells in his beak. Three minutes later the female arrived at the nest and brooded her young for about 5 minutes. Then she picked up the other eggshell and, true to form, started to eat it. But she then changed her mind and flew off with it as the male had done.

There are many instances where parent birds will swallow faecal sacs as an alternative to carrying them off but, to our knowledge, robins normally dispose of both eggshells and faecal sacs by the latter method. However, there are exceptions to this. The female parent will tend to swallow faecal sacs when the chicks are very young, e.g., just hatched. We also noticed that, if the female returns to feed the brood after a period away feeding herself or collecting food for her young, the urge to brood when she returns may sometimes be stronger than her urge to fly off with the faecal sacs. Then, and

Parent birds have two ways of disposing of faecal sacs: fly off with them or swallow them. Robins normally prefer the former method, dropping them at a safe distance from the nest. Sometimes, especially when the young are newly hatched, the female will swallow the faecal sac, presumably so that she does not need to interrupt the brooding of the chicks at their most vulnerable stage. Whichever method is used, the important thing is to remove any telltale signs to predators that there are young in the nest.

during the early part of a spell of brooding, is when she is most likely to swallow faecal sacs. Apart from these limited instances, our birds flew away with faecal sacs, disposing of them about 30 metres away. We noted a variation on the faecal sac disposal scene when photographing nesting linnets. While the parents were away collecting food, the chicks would deposit faecal sacs on the rim of the nest. Parent linnets visit the nest with food at much less frequent intervals than do insectivorous species like robins, sometimes being away for up to half an hour. The reason is that, being seedeaters, finches feed their young on regurgitated seeds. On returning to the nest, the adult would first feed the young and then collect the droppings. If there were a number of droppings to dispose of, the parent would first swallow one, or sometimes two, and then gather a further one or two in the break before flying off. We have also seen this combination waste-disposal technique adopted by robins when they have well-grown young in the nest. Incidentally, it gives an idea of the work involved in the removal of faecal sacs if you realize that

Fig 4.

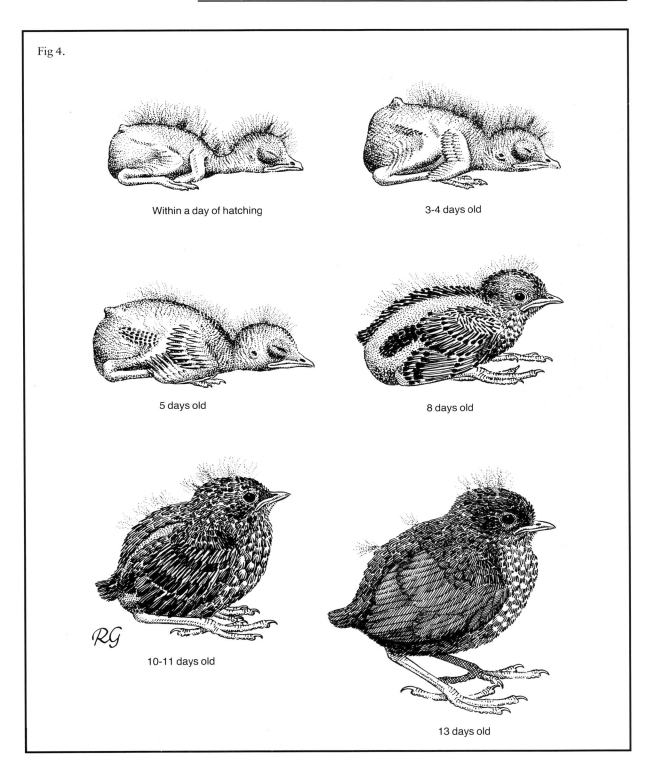

Within a day of hatching

3-4 days old

5 days old

8 days old

10-11 days old

13 days old

each chick produces about one sac an hour during the day: 4 chicks × 10 hours a day × 13 days, say, means over 500 little nappiefuls to dispose of.

The chick at birth is a naked and unlovely little thing, but begins to look more endearing as it develops. At 3 days, the quills or 'pin feathers' begin to grow but its eyes are still closed. At 5 days, the quills are longer and the eyes are partly open. Within another 2 or 3 days, tracts of feathering start to appear on the back and flanks, and the wing quills have begun to sprout at the tips, the stage known to ringers of nestlings as the 'paintbrush' stage. The eyes are now open but they have a curiously sightless look which gives the chick a dopey, dozy appearance. By about the 10th day, the body feathering, that delicious spotty brown, is quite substantial and its growth slows down. Enough of the wing feathering (the tails lags behind – no pun intended) has emerged from the 'pins' to create quite a fan, and their development into usable flight feathers is almost complete. Most striking is the change in the eyes. The dozy expression has gone, replaced by an alertness that tells you they are beginning to know what's what. The famous robin beadiness is there. Nest-recorders and other people having good reason (and a licence!) to inspect nests will be very careful from now on, because the young might become alarmed and 'explode' from the nest. At the point when they fledge, they can look quite comical. The head feathers have now grown completely, so that individual plumes stick up giving them the 'Just William' appearance of a dishevelled schoolboy who has just been pulled through a hedge backwards.

The rate of growth, and increase in weight, is affected of course by the weather and the amount of food the chicks get. Weighing in at about 1.7g on the day of its birth, the average chick will put on about another 16g in the following 10 days or so, after which the rate of increase slows, so that it will fledge at about 18.5g. Fig. 4 shows the rate of growth of a robin nestling. If there are days, such as wet and windy days, when little or no food is brought to the chicks, the evidence that this has happened is recorded on the wing and tail feathering, a phenomenon known as 'fault-barring' or 'growth-bars'. These are thin bands across the tract of flight feathers which are paler than the normal feathering because of the lack of protein during the hours that that part of the feathering continued to grow.

5   Breeding Success

Amongst the creatures that prey on birds' eggs and chicks, the hedgehog is underestimated. We have heard one clambering about, 2 metres or more up in a hedge, searching for nests. Because hedgehogs mostly hunt at night, people rarely see them in the act of predating birds' nests.

With all the effort that goes into the production of young, it is heartbreaking sometimes to consider the odds against the brood surviving. How many chicks survive depends on such factors as weather conditions; food supply; survival of both parents; and, of course, predation by such enemies as domestic cats, weasels, hedgehogs and grey squirrels, or avian predators such as jays, magpies and woodpeckers. The robin is also a host for cuckoos, ranking fifth after meadow pipit, dunnock, reed warbler and pied

It is sad that for most people in Britain nowadays, 'squirrel' means the alien grey squirrel, which is so much more intrusive and, in our view, so much less attractive than the indigenous red squirrel. Grey squirrels are probably at the top of the league of mammalian predators of birds' nests, ahead of weasels, stoats, rats and hedgehogs.

Of all the members of the crow family, the magpie is thriving best. As it has come increasingly into suburban areas, its predation of birds' nests has become more noticeable. It employs various techniques in seeking out its prey. Sometimes it moves along likely hedgerows 'cold-searching' for any signs that might lead it to a meal of eggs or chicks. On other occasions, as with the bird on the roof-top in the picture, it will take up a prominent perch and wait patiently.

wagtail. One of Martin's neighbours reported a case of squirrel predation. The nest was inside the garage. The neighbour, who was ill at the time, was watching from her window when she saw a grey squirrel go into the garage. Later, Martin found that the squirrel had eaten three of the chicks and left two others dead in the nest. Pathetically the adults continued to bring in food for the two dead young for several days, demonstrating dramatically how powerful the parental imperative really is.

It is this imperative, of course, which enables the cuckoo to parasitize, for it can be sure that the sight of the red/orange gape of its hungry chick will be enough to provoke the feeding instinct of the host parents. Once the young cuckoo has fledged and is bigger than

Another bane in the life of small birds is the risk of having to play host to a voracious cuckoo chick. To make sure that it gets all the attention, the cuckoo chick will push all the eggs or young out of the nest. Amongst garden-nesting birds, robins play host to cuckoos, but not as often as dunnocks do. The young cuckoo in the picture was being fed bits of brown bread. It would often pick up a bit of bread itself, fly to the birdbath and dunk the morsel before swallowing it.

its host parents, that blessed gape is so effective that they will often stand on its back to feed it. There are many recorded examples, too, of robins delivering their load of food not to their own young but to the young of blackbirds or greenfinches in adjacent nests, and even removing faecal sacs afterwards, as if they were at their own nest. So we should not be surprised that the pair in the garage continued to bring food even after their young were no longer alive. Martin removed the old nest and, in just over a week, the pair had rebuilt and laid a clutch of six eggs, which produced four or five young. It was an ideal nest for photography. Martin checked in the evening to see that they were all right, but when he went back next morning at 6am to do some photography, the nest was empty. His neighbour had seen nothing, but was convinced that it was the 'grey tree rat' again.

Probably the biggest culprit, as far as garden nests are concerned, is the domestic cat. It was clear, for example, that the kettle-nest had been predated by a cat, for the whole nest had been pulled out. The reaction of the pair of robins was interesting in this case, too. They remained nearby. The female constantly begged for food and the male fed her. It may have looked like 'comfort-eating', a common human reaction to life's unfairnesses, but it suggested in fact that they were already preparing for re-nesting. They were used to the inside of the shed as Mike had taken to feeding them in there and leaving a tray of mealworms for them. Next day (5 April), they started nest-building in the shed, the female as usual doing the work while her mate watched from his perch. For the next two days, the female moved to the extreme edge of the territory and lurked in the thick hedge there as if something had disturbed her at her new nest-site. We were convinced that she had deserted her new nest, but on the morning of the 10 April, we checked and, to our relief, saw the first egg in a beautifully-lined nest, which had taken only three days to build. By 15 April, there was a completed clutch of six eggs.

It is easy, and understandable, to regard the predation of young, and indeed the mortality rate after fledging, as a sad and tragic business, which, in an ideal world, would not occur. From a biological point of view, however, the mechanism is really very efficient. The object of the exercise is to ensure that the population remains stable, i.e., that as each adult dies (from whatever cause), it is replaced. Some species of bird will produce only one chick per year, because, in their particular environment, that chick is likely to survive to become a breeding adult one day. Others will produce a dozen or more per year, because, in *their* particular environment, only one is likely to survive to breeding maturity. Assuming nothing dramatic occurs (such as drastic man-made changes to their environment), the population of one-chick species like albatrosses or

A healthy brood about 12 days old. They will leave the nest within 48 hours, but would certainly 'explode', i.e., flee the nest, if disturbed by any intruder. Note how their dappled plumage enables them to merge into their background and so be less visible to predators.

multi-chick species like robins will stay the same. Unfortunately, man has often interfered with this natural balance, with the result that in many species – the larger birds of prey are a prime example – the low-level production strategy is no longer working. On the other hand, although man has interfered with the natural balance in Britain by the intentional or accidental introduction of predator species such as the grey squirrel and the mink, the predations of these aliens are not of a magnitude seriously to threaten the very survival of our birds.

But, let us return to our brood of robins. Assuming all goes well, the chicks will fledge in about 13 days from hatching. (There is a rule of thumb about the fledging time of small passerines: open-nest birds like blackbirds take about 12 days; hole-nesters like blue tits can take up to 19 days. Robins, with their partially-roofed nests, usually fledge at 12–15 days.) As with the human infant, the development of passerine chicks from naked helpless youngsters to fully-fledged, resourceful individuals is nothing short of miraculous. At birth, as we have seen, they are tiny and blind, weighing less than 2g. As they feed, their weight increases until, at fledging, they are over 18g, not much less than the weight of their parents. Their feather tracts grow very systematically, starting with the body feathering, which protects and insulates them, and finishing with the growth of their flight feathers, which gives them the necessary mobility to achieve independent existence, find their own food and avoid predators. And all this in a fortnight!

'Last one out's a cissy!' This robin's brothers and sisters have already left the nest, encouraged by the calls of the parents, and are concealed in nearby vegetation. With the nest abandoned, there is no longer any need to worry about telltale signs of occupancy, hence the dropping below the nest. If you find an empty nest, you can usually tell whether the young have left safely because of droppings in and around the nest, and because the rim, where the chicks stood plucking up courage before take-off, becomes flattened.

The moment of fledging is dramatic, but one is rarely privileged to see it in the case of well-concealed nesters like the robin. There is a great deal of agitation as the surviving young stretch and exercise, experiment with wing-flapping, frequently preening to help rid each growing feather of the remains of its waxy sheath, and generally rev up their engines for the big take-off. Often they have to take it in turns to go through these routines because there is not enough room for them all to do it simultaneously. Eventually, the big day arrives. They stand on the lip of the nest, crowding and jostling, while the parent birds call encouragingly from nearby. By the time all the offspring have sprung off, as it were, the lip of the nest is not only flattened, but also covered with their droppings (no need for the hygienic and cautious removal of the faecal sac any more), and this flattening and careless toilet are sure signs that the young have successfully fledged.

Once they are out of the nest and safely, if somewhat uncertainly, perched on a nearby twig, the young wait expectantly to be fed. After all, this is how life has been up to this moment. The parent birds will oblige for a time, triggered by the begging calls of their young and, on occasions, by the begging calls of other species' young. From aviary

Juveniles will normally stay hidden and wait for food to be brought to them, but they will occasionally approach the parent birds who are at or near a good food supply. The parents, egged on by the incessant begging calls of their young, will continue to feed the chicks out of the nest for about 3 weeks. Fledged young of the first brood will tend to be fed more by the male while the female gets on with the business of starting a second family.

studies, it seems that chicks will start to become independent, seeking their own food, after about 21 days, but the truth is that the parents, or at least the female, at a certain point will become less interested in the fledged young of their last brood and much more concerned with starting the next.

In a good year, robins will have two or even three broods (not counting repeats after a nest has been predated). In one nest-box, lovingly constructed and erected in an orchard as part of our attempt to increase the number of nesting spotted flycatchers, a pair of robins took up residence and were so prolific that we were able to ring 13 pulli (young) from three broods in the same nest-box – and not a runt amongst them.

Talking of nest-boxes, we are still looking for an answer to the question: do you need to remove the old nest to encourage second and third broods in the same season? Mike reports that his parents had a nest-box in which robins nested every year, raising one brood, which was nearly always successful, but never using it for a second brood. He decided one year to remove the nest within a day or two of the young leaving in the hope of encouraging the pair to use it for a second brood. Within three days they were rebuilding in the same nest-box and raised a second brood. Conversely, in the orchard nest-box referred to above, the robins raised 13 young from three broods without the old nest being pulled out by us. Even this can be topped by a Fordingbridge nest-box sited inside a greenhouse. It produced 14 young from four broods. The old nest was not pulled out, but the facts of the case are probably distorted because food was being put out, mostly the crumbly Cheshire cheese referred to elsewhere.

All we can say is that it may be advisable to clear out old nests from nest-boxes after the end of the breeding season as they are likely to harbour parasites and/or become foetid through decay. Many nest-box users will do it themselves if you don't do it for them. Blue tits and starlings, for example, have been observed 'spring-cleaning', i.e., removing the old nesting material from a box before building a fresh nest in there.

6 Food and Feeding Habits

Robins are primarily insectivorous, feeding in the summer mainly on the caterpillars of butterflies and moths, such as the silver–y moth, and the larvae of many other species. Robins will chase and catch butterflies, but they tend to let them go, finding them unpleasant for some reason. In the winter, they will become more dependent on non-insect food, but still manage to find likely prey, especially beetles, including rove beetles like the Devil's coach-horse. And whenever such items are available, they will also gobble up ladybirds and weevils; earwigs, sawflies, ants and gall-insects; and other kinds of flies, such as the house fly and its eggs and larvae. They are partial to a snack of spiders, centipedes or earthworms too, and will go in for seed- and berry-eating, including ivy and hawthorn berries, when the going gets tough in the cold season. A note in the November 1984 issue of *British Birds* records a robin tearing off and eating pieces of a gilled fungus, which, contrary to expectations, had no invertebrate infestation. Robins are indeed opportunist feeders. Moreover, because of their large light-gathering eyes, they tend to start hunting earlier in the day than other small birds, and are still looking for supper when the light has all but gone. (If you want to throw out some cheese and you want to be sure that it goes to the robins, do so just before dusk, when the starlings and house sparrows have retired for the night.)

As most of their prey is live, their typical tactic is to perch low in a hedge or other vegetation, maybe half a metre to a metre or so from the ground, and watch out for movement, at which point they will fly out or down to snatch a tasty morsel. Once they have done this, they have disturbed the site and so will move on to another part of their territory and repeat the process. They are lucky, because they know that there is plenty more 'live pudding' in every part of their patch. In other words, they can repeat the process endlessly, returning to a perch once the previous disturbance has been forgotten. It can be quite amusing to see how a robin copes when it lands on an unstable perch: say, a slender twig that turns out to be bouncy. Its head will remain still while the rest of its body moves to compensate for the movement of the perch. In this way, like a hovering kestrel, it keeps

its eye steady whatever the rest of its body may be doing.

There are even some startling records of robins using the perch-and-pounce technique to catch fish. David Lack, for example, recorded robins catching 'minnows for their young from a brook which had nearly dried up'. Perhaps the most extraordinary case however was the one reported in the December 1987 issue of *BBC Wildlife* magazine, based on the observations and photography of Robert Gross, who lives in Fulda, Germany. Gross had been photographing kingfishers at the same site for several seasons before a robin started to appear regularly and, after a time, decided to have a go. It started by flying down to the water's edge, after the kingfisher had made its plunge, trying to catch one of the fish that had fled to the shallows. On one occasion, the robin (Gross was sure it was always the same bird) even sat on the same branch as its mentor. One day, the robin almost literally took the plunge: it began hovering over the water to drive fish into the shallows. Eventually it developed a heron-like technique, standing motionless in the water, often up to its breast, and grabbing any passing fish. Gross saw it catch 15 fish in a single day, using this technique. Its method of despatching a fish

A robin will hunt from any convenient perch within its territory. Birds perching on washing lines, as in this photograph, are to be discouraged on days when the washing is hanging out to dry!

There are a number of records of small songbirds taking fish, including a wren which became a nuisance at a trout farm when it persisted in snaffling fry. But nothing can beat this robin, which took lessons from a kingfisher and quickly learned how to take fish which had been driven into the shallows.

Robins are very happy to let someone else do the work, and will stay close to anyone (even moles!) turning the soil and exposing worms and other morsels. In this shot, the gardener has also provided a convenient perch from which the bird, its beady eye wide open, will spot the slightest movement on the freshly-dug ground below.

was simple and effective: it would beat it senseless on a branch before swallowing it whole, head first. Only the larger fish were slippery and wriggly enough to get away. Wrens have been known to poach trout fry, and thrushes will sometimes nobble a tadpole or two, but for sheer ingenuity and audacity, Gross's robin takes some beating.

The robin's close association with man opens the door to all sorts of other possibilities. We heard of one family — a pair of robins with their single surviving youngster — coming regularly to a patio to feed on Cheshire cheese, supplied deliberately by the obliging human occupants of the house. One supposes that they had experimented with the cheeseboard before plumping for Cheshire, which 'is better because it crumbles easily'. Robins, like human beings, can be faddy,

We must come clean about this photograph. Mike is a very reluctant gardener, and only stuck his spade into the ground to get this shot. A nearby supply of mealworms lured the robin, Tame, into camera range, at which point Mike fired the camera using a long cable release.

90

though. Martin noticed differences in feeding habits in winter-feeding. The first robin ate mealworms and pupae, but the one which replaced it was very nervous and only took the occasional mealworm.

Martin also had an interesting experience of what you might call inadvertent feeding. To quote his field notes:

> One day I dug up a red ants' nest. The bird, which had earlier been coming to my hand to take mealworms, flew down to pick some pupae which had been exposed, but after a short while it flew away to pick off the ants which were swarming over its legs. After that, it would not go back to the ants' nest, not even when I put some mealworms on it to tempt it.

Every gardener knows that robins are opportunist feeders, down at your feet to grab a morsel almost before your spade has turned the soil over. But human beings are not the only 'gardeners' to provide a free digging service for the robin. There is a lovely report in the February 1982 issue of *British Birds* in which the magazine's editor describes how he watched a mole raising lines of soil across his lawn in the course of constructing shallow tunnels. The industrious mole was followed by a grateful robin, which managed to devour one or two worms before being displaced by two blackbirds. An aspect of the story which is even more surprising than the robin's enterprise is the calm with which the editor contemplated the mole in the act of digging up his lawn. Most of us would have been furious!

7   Post-breeding Activities

Wing held open showing final stages of wing moult. The new feathers emerge from a waxy sheath, as can be seen at the base of the small outer feathers and the new secondaries. The moult of different tracts of flight feathers is staggered to retain optimum mobility.

The name of the game is survival. The first priority for any bird after the search for food and shelter is the maintenance of plumage, i.e., the body feathering which keeps it warm, and the flight feathers of wing and tail which give it mobility and manoeuvrability. The plumage is replaced annually by the process known as moulting. Different kinds of birds go about moult in different ways. Birds of prey, for example, which cannot afford to have their flight ability

impaired, are in continuous moult of their flight feathers, which is why you so often notice gaps in their wings or tail where a new feather is growing. (New central tail feathers emerging on a marsh harrier's tail can produce a forked appearance and a mis-identification of the harrier as a black or red kite by the unwary.) Ducks, geese and swans can lose all their flight feathers simultaneously and thus become flightless for about a month. Passerines generally have a progressive moult which does not impair their activities too much but which is likely all the same to cause them to tuck themselves out of harm's way. Our late colleague, Mike Webber, posed the question one day: where do all the adult great tits go in August? After a lot of investigation in Wytham Wood near Oxford, he discovered that they all go up to the tops of trees while they moult, out of sight and out of danger. Similarly, there is a period of about 4–5 weeks during the summer when you are lucky to see any adult robins: they are all skulking in the bottom of the hedgerows while they moult. Although they look for all the world as if they were ashamed to be seen because of their ragged, half-moulted appearance, the fact of the matter is that they are *hors de combat*: the temporary

Ragged robin – not the flower, but a bird in head moult. The waxy sheaths from which the new feathering emerges are clearly visible in this picture. Robins in August, when the main moult occurs, are conspicuous by their absence, as they tend to hide themselves away.

lack of a fine red breast means that they do not have the wherewithal to announce and defend a territory.

The sequence of moult is common to most passerines. The ten primary flight feathers are dropped in sequence starting with the innermost one, i.e., the moult starts in the middle of the wing and moves to the edge. Both wings moult at the same rate and in the same sequence. After about four or five primaries have dropped, the next to start are the three feathers nearest the body. Although they are effectively part of the tract known as the secondaries, they are called tertials; the German name for them, *Schirmfedern*, meaning 'protective feathers', gives a much better description of their function as they are the topmost feathers on the closed wing, the ones which protect the others. Then, when there are still about five primaries to go, the remaining six feathers (i.e., the main tract of the secondaries) start to moult from the outermost (i.e., in the middle of the wing) to the innermost. At the same time, the 12 tail feathers start to moult in pairs, usually from the middle pair outwards. The moult of the flight feathers is so timed that the tail moult is completed before the growth of the last wing feather. Diagrammatically, the moult of flight feathers looks like this:

Primaries (1–10)	1	2	3	4	5	6	7	8	9	10
Secondaries (1–6)					1	2	3	4	5	6
Tertials (7–9)					8	9	7			
Tail (in pairs)						1	2	3	4	5 6

Moult of the coverts and the body and head feathering starts during the moult of flight feathers and continues afterwards, the whole process taking between 50 and 60 days. Interesting as it is to see an adult robin looking ragged, robin moult is observed at its most dramatic in the transformation of the juveniles. Unlike the adults, which have a complete moult of body and flight feathers, juveniles of most passerine species only moult the body feathering, i.e., that of the body, head and smaller wing-coverts. In the robin, the change in appearance is spectacular. They emerge as fledgelings with a dappled or speckled spotty-brown plumage, which has a considerable camouflage value at a time of year when woodlands are bathed in dappled sunlight. Their late-summer post-juvenile moult produces a complete transformation, into a plumage which is virtually indistinguishable from the adult's, except for buff tips to the greater coverts which soon wear away. During this period of transformation, they can look most appealing as the red progressively replaces the speckled breast feathering. Chris Mead, in his book *Robins*, describes how the orange breast colour starts from the upper centre

Now that the juvenile's need for cryptic dappled plumage has diminished, it will begin to moult into adult plumage. This individual has started by growing its first two red feathers at the base of the breast.

and spreads outwards and downwards, but our observations suggest that this is not always so: all the juveniles we photographed were producing the red feathering from the bottom of the breast upwards, while another juvenile was seen to have red only on the forehead. By mid-October the process is complete and you will be hard-pressed to tell a juvenile from an adult, even in the hand.

For all this attention to survival, the robin, in common with other small passerines, has a short life expectancy, with most lucky to enjoy more than one breeding season. As to longevity for the hardy – or lucky – minority, in ringing recoveries of over 5000 birds, the oldest robin was 8½ years old. Just as well, too, for, as we discussed earlier, only enough young need to survive to keep the population at the same level: if the majority of all young robins born were to survive beyond their first year, we would soon be up to the armpits in robins.

A juvenile moult well under way. The red breast is almost complete; throat and forehead will be the next to take on the familiar adult hue.

96

So what kills them off?

The North Wind will blow
And we shall have Snow
And what will the Robin do then, poor thing?
He'll sit in the Barn to keep himself warm
And hide his Head under his Wing, poor thing.

Most small birds die from natural causes, usually starvation or disease. Amongst the many ways in which robins meet an untimely end, road casualties account for about one death in ten. Since roadside hedgerows are a prime habitat, this is not surprising. The most frequently reported cause of death, though, is 'killed by cat', accounting for almost a quarter of all recorded fatalities – the price paid by robins for being so fond of gardens and other human habitations.

Cold weather is a killer, especially when an animal becomes susceptible as a result of difficulty in getting enough food to stay in trim. If you asked the average man in the street what caused the most deaths in robins and other small birds, he would probably say: 'Killed by cats or hit by cars'. If he was a birdwatcher, he might think of the toll taken by owls or sparrowhawks (actually less than 2 per

Wheeling flocks of starlings, tightly grouped, can betray the presence of a bird of prey. With the continuing increase in their numbers, sparrowhawks can often be seen flying over or hunting through gardens. This wary robin was watching an aircraft which it obviously perceived as predator-shaped.

99

This photograph was taken in a woodland setting. Sparrowhawks and robins were both originally woodland species, so the latter must appear on the former's menu quite frequently. The increase of sparrowhawks in gardens reflects the fact that these birds of prey are thriving again after becoming all but extinct in the fifties as a result of pesticide poisoning.

cent of reported deaths). If he had had the experience of Martin, who found a robin that was killed when it flew into a glass panel in the back porch, leaving a 'ghost image' on the glass, he might give windows as a cause too. (Actually, according to BTO figures, less than 1 per cent of reported deaths occur in this way.) In each case, he would be reflecting the causes of death reported to the BTO by people finding ringed birds. (Cats account for about 25 per cent of reported deaths, road casualties for about 10 per cent.) One particularly bizarre accident was reported by our friend, Paul Mason of Haddenham, Ely:

Death by collision with the glass of a window or patio door accounts for very few robins' sudden demise – probably less than one in a hundred reported deaths – but it can leave a marked impression: literally, as this picture shows. The ghostly outline of the bird left on the glass is caused by the oils and dust in its feathering.

We had a robin once that became very elusive after having entered through the kitchen door. One moment it was there, then it wasn't. Either it was hiding away cowering in fright, which I didn't really believe, or it was poking around for food behind the cupboards somewhere. It didn't reappear, so we finally decided that it must have gone outside again without our noticing. It was only later that my wife found it in a mousetrap, which it had entered having taken a fancy to the cheese bait.

A startling calculation made by David Harper in his study of robins at Cranborne in Dorset, and reported in the BBC's wildlife film, *Who Really Killed Cock Robin?*, is that one in eleven robins is killed by another robin in the course of territorial disputes. But the fact is that the majority of birds die of cold, starvation or disease, and we are much less likely to find those birds.

Small birds in cold weather often look very plump, not because they have put on weight, but because they have fluffed out their feathers to provide an insulating layer of trapped air on the string vest principle. The bird had to be photographed using flash, otherwise it would have appeared as a silhouette with the rising sun beyond.

The state of the weather is expressed by the frosted leaves of a cotoneaster, and confirmed by this robin puffing its feathers out against the cold. At such times, robins will often stand on one leg or adopt a squatting position to reduce heat loss through the legs.

8   Movement and Migration

Robins are not renowned as long-distance migrants, although some races do move from their breeding territories to more hospitable parts in southerly or south-westerly regions of the Continent in the winter. For example, ringing recoveries suggest that most Scandinavian robins migrate, as do a substantial proportion of German birds.

In fact, scientists, using this movement of Continental robins, have been able to make a substantial contribution to our knowledge and understanding of the mysterious mechanisms of migration. For example, a report in the October 1979 issue of *British Birds* describes how, in the 1960s, some German scientists used robins in experiments to discover how far birds made use of information from the earth's magnetic field in migration. The scientists discovered that the orientation of robins in circular test cages (where no visual clues were available) could be changed in a predictable way by rotating the magnetic field, for example, by making magnetic north in the cage coincide with magnetic east.

Although, our own British robins are best regarded as sedentary, there are movements within the country, and very occasionally to the Continent. Thirty years of ringing data from Hengistbury Head, which is a promontory on the south coast of Dorset and a famous migration point, provide only two foreign recoveries (out of ten, the other eight being local, mostly of the 'killed by cat' variety):

A brief moment of indignity and indignation as a robin is ringed. The ring, which bears a unique combination of letters and numbers, gives the bird an individual identity if and when it is trapped again by another ringer or recovered (the term used for the finding of a dead bird). Ringing also provides an opportunity to gather other information from the bird in the hand, for example by weighing it and recording moult.

Ring number			
AA70481	Ad	Hengistbury	04.09.60
	x	Renuhec en St-Nolff, Brittany, France	22.09.60
F117231	3	Hengistbury	29.08.88
	x	Guengat, Finisterre, France	27.01.89

Even the Guengat bird was 'tué par un chat'!
N.B. Ad = adult; 3 = hatched during calendar year of ringing; x = found dead

All the robin ringing data from the BTO provides no more than a score of recoveries of British-ringed robins overseas, of which the most spectacular is a bird ringed as a nestling in Wales and recovered

British robins are fairly sedentary creatures, but there is evidence of long-distance movement and migration, especially by females, after the breeding season. The best place to see robins on the move is at the coast. The promontory in this picture is Hengistbury Head in Dorset but the robin overflying it is not migrating anywhere – all is revealed in Chapter 10.

105

about 8 months later 1600km away in Spain (typically, it had been shot). Chris Mead, estimating the number of robins migrating to the Continent, says: 'If pressed, I would guess that it was less than 5 per cent of females and probably hardly any males.' As he is the Head of the BTO Ringing Scheme, it would be as well to take his word for it.

But robins do move about outside the breeding season. One autumn, a Hengistbury ringer, the late Mike Webber, wanted to study territoriality in robins, so he set about catching and colour-ringing all the robins in the area. He started in September, estimating that about 12–15 pairs of robins had bred in the study area that summer. Clearly he needed to trap and ring every robin if his results were to have any meaning. Fortunately Mike was a very determined fellow, and he was very successful in catching robins, both in mist nets and in ground-traps. But, to his astonishment, he found that he had soon used up all the colour combinations available to him – about 50 – and that he was *still* catching robins every day throughout the autumn. Worse, only very few of his colour-ringed robins were ever seen again. What *was* going on? It finally dawned on him, and the rest of us, that very few of the robins which he had caught were in fact Hengistbury residents. (These few were the ones that were seen subsequently by observers.) The majority were simply passing through, 'coasting', just as other common species like greenfinches do outside the breeding season! At least Mike found out something that nobody had suspected before, namely that hundreds of robins passed through the area in the course of the winter. So, when people who live and have gardens near coastal areas, talk about 'our Robin', they could be looking at a different individual each day. A similar phenomenon occurs with other species visiting garden-feeders in winter.

People who regularly go birdwatching on the east coast in Autumn are keen weather buffs: they know that a certain combination can produce a spectacular arrival of birds from across the North Sea – what is called a 'fall'. The late Eric Hosking, in his book *An Eye for a Bird*, gives a wonderful description of such a fall:

[We] realised that something unusual was happening and so we hurried to the observation hut . . . . Birds were everywhere, the place was alive with them . . . . In all, between 1.15pm and dusk, we recorded fifty-two species along a three-quarter mile front [including] 4000 Wheatears, 750 Whinchats, 7000 Redstarts, 400 Robins, 2000 Garden Warblers, 200 Whitethroats, 500 Willow Warblers, 300 Spotted Flycatchers, 1500 Pied Flycatchers and 150 Tree Pipits.

A similar fall of Scandinavian migrants on 11 October 1982,

reported in the August 1985 issue of *British Birds*, estimates that 4000 Robins landed on the Isle of May (in the Firth of Forth) alone. Wow! We ourselves were lucky enough to be at Thornham Point just to the west of Titchwell on the north Norfolk coast one morning in late October 1990, when the weather conditions were ideal for such a phenomenon. And we were not disappointed. Birds from Scandinavia were swept in on the easterly winds circling the bottom of the high pressure zone over that region, and then pulled down by the thick fog which swirled over the English coast, the interface between the Scandinavian high and a typical British low pressure system. As the day got lighter, we became aware of lots of goldcrests dropping on to the sand dunes all around us. It is an uncanny and privileged feeling to have dozens of these tiny birds running between your feet or feeding unconcernedly within centimetres of you. By the end of the morning the number of goldcrests that had made landfall must have been in the thousands. In a way even more exciting for us were the numbers of robins that came in. It seemed as if every bush and shrub had a robin in or under it. Our count of robins was creeping towards the second hundred when we decided to move on, attracted – distracted might be a better word – by other delights, including redwings, bramblings and other finches as well as a party of a dozen or so late blackcaps. It would be nice to report that we managed to distinguish the robins as 'Continental' on the basis of their greyer backs and their paler orange breasts. To tell the truth, we tried to, but couldn't be sure, mainly because the dull mistiness of the morning seemed to lend such a ghostly pale cast to everything round us, including these tired migrants.

We have said that British robins do not move very far, but this statement needs qualification. All the evidence is that *male* robins do not move very far, but there is a dearth of *females* outside the breeding season. David Lack's study in south Devon suggested that between 60 and 75 per cent of female robins migrate, or at least leave the area, whereas only a small number of males move out, and those are mostly first-year birds. Interestingly, the females who remain become very 'masculine' in their behaviour, for, as we have noted earlier, they fight and sing and defend their territory every bit as stoutly as the males. This winter dearth of females is not confined to the wintertime. In fact, even in the breeding season, after the wandering females have returned, there are never enough to go round. (This leads to some fairly desperate and despicable extramarital adventuring on the part of unattached males, but that is another story.) The great unanswered question is: where do the females go after the breeding season? Nobody knows: even our most familiar garden bird has yet to give up all its secrets.

9 Robins and People

The lives of man and robins are inextricably linked. This is shown by a number of things, not the least of which is the way some individual robins can become ridiculously tame. It is presumably an extension of a fundamental quality of the robin, its restless curiosity and determination to investigate closely anything strange and new that it meets. E. M. Nicholson, in his book *Birds and Men* (1951), quotes the time when he saw:

> a Robin, on the way to feed a brood with a beakful of insects, turn aside on hearing the cry of a Wryneck, and flit up to the top of an oak to quiz the stranger from a perch within a couple of feet of him.

Cry of a wryneck? Those were the days!

He also gives another example of this nosiness:

> Another singing on a fence broke off to drop to the ground for a ringside view of a fierce fight between two cock Chaffinches which came down together locked in duel.

We were able to exploit the robin's propensity to investigate – and its well-known weakness for mealworms – to lure robins into focus, so to speak. The one that Mike christened Tame became so bold that he was able to hand-feed it. Mike would hold out the tin containing mealworms and tap the side of it, and, in the best Pavlovian tradition, Tame would fly down from the fence, perch on the edge of the tin, extract a mealworm and then fly back to the fence to enjoy its meal. After Tame, who turned out to be a male, found a mate, Mike hoped to make her hand-tame too, but she was shy, venturing no nearer than about six metres. Slowly she became more confident, and eventually became brazen enough, by her standards, to collect mealworms put down about two metres away. A friend of ours had a robin that became so relaxed and confident that it not only took mealworms from his hand, but would also use it occasionally as a song-perch.

The very name of the bird underlines the important place it holds in our affections. To us, a robin is a robin. To a scientist, it is

Tame waiting for his customary snack of mealworms. Some robins regularly venture inside houses in search of food. Tame would occasionally do this, but on the whole he had us much better trained: *we* went to *him* with food.

Erithacus rubecula (from the Greek *erythros* meaning 'red'; and the Latin *ruber* meaning 'reddish'). We used to call it redbreast or ruddock (just as 'dunnock' means 'dun-coloured', so 'ruddock' means 'reddish-coloured') and, in the same way, its colour makes it *broindergh* ('red belly') in Gaelic and *yr fron goch* ('red bird') in Welsh. So where did 'robin' come from? Robin is a first or Christian name, a diminutive or variant of Robert; the habit of giving familiar birds a first name used to be widespread amongst country folk. Some

The BTO Garden Bird Feeding Survey has revealed that robins are among the most frequent visitors to feeding-stations, along with blackbirds, blue and great tits, house sparrows, dunnocks and greenfinches. Robins, like the one in this picture (left), find grated cheese irresistible.

we can still remember, like Jenny Wren and Tom Tit, even though they have fallen into disuse. Some are long dead, or survive only in dialect, such as the vernacular names listed in *British Birds, Eggs and Nests Popularly Described* by Reverend J. C. Atkinson (1870): Nanny wagtail (pied wagtail), King Harry redcap (goldfinch), Willy Wicket (common sandpiper), Madge or Gilly Howlet and Jenny Howlet (barn owl and tawny owl respectively), Bessy Ducker (dipper), Billy Biter (blue tit) and Jack Baker (red-backed shrike: to think it was once common enough to have a local name!). Other first names have become incorporated into the bird's current name, like Jack Daw into jackdaw and Madge or Mag Pie into magpie.

In the case of the Robin Redbreast, only its first name, Robin, has survived. Curiously, in parts of Scotland, another first name is prefixed to Robin, giving the endearing variation 'Bob Robin', which could equally be descriptive of the bird's alert bobbing movements. Just as curious is the fact that it was only in 1952 that the name robin, instead of redbreast, was finally accepted by the British Ornithologists' Union. (This is the arbiter in the matter of vernacular names. In 1988, the BOU proposed further changes, whereby robin will become European robin. If the long-tailed tit is renamed as the long-tailed bush-tit, the bearded tit as the bearded parrotbill, and the

Tame (right) started by taking mealworms from a hand-held tin. Once he became confident, he was happy to take them from the hand. Both pictures show him frozen in mid-flight using high-speed flash. The lower picture shows his wings bent to give drag and his undercarriage out ready for landing.

dunnock as the hedge accentor, we will have them to thank — or curse, depending on your point of view.)

In her wonderful book about the names, lore and literature of British birds, *All the Birds of the Air* (1973), Francesca Greenoak has also collected these dialect names for the robin: 'Thomas Gierdet' and 'Tommy-liden', though goodness knows what inspired them. She also notes that in parts of Yorkshire it is known as the 'Ploughman's Bird'.

Stories about the robin abound in folklore and legend. Everyone knows how the robin got its red breast. A robin was plucking thorns from Christ's crown, pricked itself and the blood stained its breast. Right? Of course — unless you belong to the Bringing-of-Fire School of Thought, in which case you will know that the robin, while in the process of bringing fire to man, accidentally scorched its breast feathers. If you subscribe to the Wren-as-Bringer-of-Fire School of Thought, legend provides a useful variation: the robin took over from the wren on the way and accidentally scorched its breast, presumably because it was less careful than the wren . . .

The legend about the wound caused by the thorn in Christ's terrible crown fits in well with the association of the robin with Christianity. Indeed, the affection in which we hold the robin goes back centuries, and possibly pre-dates the Christian era. Affection, and perhaps apprehension too, for it was widely held that dreadful things would happen to anyone who harmed or killed a robin: accidents, illness, even death. Conversely, the robin is seen as the embodiment of Christian charity, as in the poignant moment — quoted in Francesca Greenoak's book — in *Babes in the Wood*, when the children have frozen to death:

No burial this pretty pair
From any man receives
Till Robin Redbreast piously
Covers them with leaves.

She also quotes from Drayton's poem, 'The Owle', published in 1604:

Covering with moss the dead's unclosed eye,
The little Redbreast teacheth Charity.

But it is the robin's association with Christmas that is most striking. Often the drawings are, anatomically speaking, appallingly inaccurate, but it doesn't matter at all. Whatever the artist's style — careful-realistic, comical or geometrical-abstract — he or she seems to capture instantly the essential 'robinness' of the bird: a feathery bundle perfectly sphere-shaped, with a splash of red (or pink or

Why is the robin so closely associated with Christmas? Because of the legend that it pulled the thorns from Christ's crown (and scratched itself in the process, spilling blood on its breast)? Because the first red-jacketed postmen, bringers of Christmas presents, were called 'robins'? Or simply because it is hard to think of a snow scene without a robin in it? Whatever the reason, the Christmas tree in the picture seems to form a perfect backdrop for the robin.

orange or vermilion . . .), a bright beady eye, and a long-legged upright stance. Every bird has its characteristic but indefinable appearance, usually known as 'jizz' (the word was used by aeroplane spotters in the Second World War). If you ever need to exemplify the word 'jizz' to non-birding friends, show them a stack of Christmas cards. Even the silliest Christmas robin standing on a snow-bedecked doorstep, with a scarf round its neck and a letter in its beak (did you know, by the way, that the first postmen were called 'robins' because they wore a red uniform?), still, amazingly, *looks* like a robin. Now that's character.

A bird has arrived socially when it is used as a heraldic device in coats of arms. There are eagles and falcons a-plenty in all sorts of postures – rousant, soaring, volant, displayed. There are noble pelicans, swans and ostriches. There are birds providing puns on family names: corbie (crow) for the Corbetts, larks for the Clarkes, hirondelles (swallows) for Arundel. There is the martlet, defined in Boutell's *Heraldry* as a 'legless swallow', used as the mark of the fourth son. There is even the inelegantly named 'dunghill cock' – and they are welcome to it – on the Alcock escutcheon. But the poor old robin seems to have been overlooked. The only heraldic representation of a robin we know of is on the Glasgow City coat of arms, commemorating a rather dubious legend about a bishop who resurrected a dead robin by breathing on it piously. But the ubiquity of the robin on Christmas cards and as a symbol or trade mark for all sorts of things from starch to three-wheeler cars, and from nursery schools to Swindon Town Football Club, more than makes up for its failure to arrive socially in the heraldic armorial. After all, who actually *looks* at coats of arms?

10 Photographing the Robin

We used single lens reflex cameras and a variety of lenses, ranging from 28mm and 50mm (e.g., for the birds in the hanging basket shown on page 62) to 400mm. In fact we used the 400mm lenses for most of the photography. Not surprisingly, the camera was nearly always supported on a heavy tripod or on a bean bag on the car window. Kodachrome 64 film was used for all the photography. Slow-speed film is essential if you are intending to publish your photographs, since with faster films you lose resolution and sharpness. Another essential in many situations was the use of flash. Birds move fast, and robins are no exception. To quote from E. M. Nicholson again, referring to the robin's reaction to danger:

> one which I was watching . . . reacted so fast to the sudden discharge of a gun within a hundred yards, that his form looked quite blurred as he instantly dashed for cover.

While blurring can legitimately be used to suggest speed, you usually wish to avoid it, hence the flash. The bird can still beat you, though: we wish we had a pound for every slide that ended up in the waste-paper bin because we so often caught the action just out of the area lit by flash. Flash is also a frequent necessity when you are photographing nesting birds, especially with species that tend to nest in darkish places, as the robin does. We prefer not to use flash* if we can avoid it as natural light looks softer and provides better modelling (shadows, which emphasize details, contours and relief), especially in the early morning and late evening. Natural light also has the advantage that you don't need to carry it with you! But we have to concede that flash allows us to work during dull weather, and gives a constant amount of light when the ambient light conditions are variable, a constant feature of the seasons in Britain.

When we mention that we use flash, some people express the feeling that flash must disturb the bird in some way. The loud click of

---

* There is a way to alleviate the inevitable harshness inherent in flash, namely, the use of a diffuser.

the camera as it fires is, of course, another potential source of disturbance. Whilst it would be true to say that clicks and flashes cause some reaction in the birds, if the preparatory work is done correctly, birds will accept things fairly readily.

We are thinking particularly of the care that must be taken when setting up for photography: introducing the hide gradually by bringing it closer over a period of days; always checking the reaction to each new situation; always being prepared to pull out if there is any sign at all of an adverse reaction; having a 'walker-away' when entering the hide, and so on. The walker-away stratagem works like this: two of you go to the hide, one of you enters and remains while the other walks away, thus fooling the bird, who cannot count higher than one presumably, into thinking that all human presence has gone. We have been told by farmers that some birds, especially members of the crow family, can count to two, so it may be necessary to send in *three* people and have *two* walk away. Eric Hosking, in his book *An Eye for a Bird*, recounts how, when photographing ravens at the nest, he tried that two-in-one-out method but the ravens were not fooled. He waited an hour and a half inside the hide while the ravens wheeled round refusing to settle. He solved the problem by recruiting a class of 30 schoolchildren out on a nature ramble. The whole class accompanied him to the hide and then walked back down. The ravens, mathematically outwitted, were back on their nest within minutes.

The disturbance argument is plausible, and we respect people for raising the issue, for it shows that they share our view that the welfare of the bird is paramount in photography as in any other kind of ornithological activity. The fact is, however, that, while excessive disturbance could have serious consequences, birds quickly become used to the clicks and flashes from the equipment rather in the way that people living by a railway line cease to notice the trains going by.

Our concern for the welfare of the bird is not merely our view: it is enshrined in law. You need a special permit to photograph some birds at the nest. A number of vulnerable British species are specially protected, so that you need to have a separate permit for each individual species: and even to approach the nest of such a bird without a permit renders you liable to hefty fines, and rightly so.

We used hides a great deal, mainly to ensure that the birds were reacting to each other rather than to our presence. The problem with hides, of course, is that they are static and presuppose that the subject will be there and do what you want it to, sooner or later. While this is generally true for nest-photography, you have to be more ingenious in order to capture other aspects of the bird's life and activities. In effect, you have sometimes to 'manipulate' your subject. The art of

The way to a robin's heart is through its stomach. We used mealworms – just about the robin's favourite food – to tame various robins in an effort to get them coming within camera range. Technical note for the self-employed: mealworms bred and used for this purpose are tax-allowable!

photography is either being in the right place at the right time, hoping that the equipment works and that nothing moves too fast for the shutter speed you have set, or creating the right activity where you are set up. For example, putting out mealworms regularly modified the birds' behaviour or encouraged them to stay in a certain place longer. In the robin-and-gardener shot on page 90, there is a tray of mealworms just beyond the robin . . . but out of sight. The camera has a 28mm lens and there is a cable release held by the gardener.

A more elaborate example of what you might call 'managed' photography is the shot on page 105 of a robin flying over Hengistbury Head. Clearly you cannot stand out in the middle of the English Channel waiting for a robin to fly past, so you have to 'stage' the event. This is how it was done. We started with a shot of Hengistbury Head which we had in stock, and made a large print of it. This constituted the background. Next, the camera was positioned on a high tripod and aimed at the Hengistbury Head print. To the left was a glass-fronted release box, with its exit to the right, so that the bird on release would fly in front of the Hengistbury Head print. Two flash guns were aimed at the Hengistbury Head print and two at the bird's flight line. (A very short duration of flash effectively freezes the bird in flight.)

But first, as Mrs Beeton might have said, harpoon your robin. We have to thank John Morgan and his colleagues of the Christchurch Harbour Ringing Station for allowing us to be present during ringing operations at their Constant Effort Site, and for being clever enough to predict that they would, sooner or later, catch a robin. They did – eventually – and were kind enough to free it from our release-box so that we could get our shot. As the bird flew out of the release-box, it broke an infra-red beam. Complicated electronic circuitry fired the camera, which in turn fired the flash guns. And there you are (you hope): an action shot of a bird 'flying over Hengistbury Head' – without getting your feet wet!

We also used the infra-red beam technique to get the shot of a bird in flight to the hand on page 111. By the use of mealworms, the bird was encouraged to perch on a spade-handle. Once it got used to this, the photographer walked round and held out the mealworms in the pre-arranged spot. On its way to the food, the robin flew through the beam, thus firing the camera.

The photograph of Mike with a robin perched on the end of a 400mm lens (page 24) was a set-up job too. Mike was on his own, in fact, so he had to set up a second tripod-mounted camera with a 100mm lens which was pre-focused on the first camera. The robin, our old friend Tame, was encouraged to perch on the 400mm lens with a bribe of mealworms and, when it did so, Mike looked into his camera and at the same time fired the second camera with a long electric-release cable.

We freely admit, though, that photographers sometimes become so ingenious in their efforts to manage the subject that their activities border on farce. For instance, we knew we would be extremely lucky to be ready just at the moment when a territorial boundary dispute between males occurred. Worse still, even if you know where a dispute is likely to occur, the location of the dispute may be

The problem with befriending a robin for photographic purposes by, for example, feeding it mealworms is that it can become too bold. In this case, instead of behaving as is required for a good natural shot it came and perched on the spare camera as if to say, 'OK, where's my breakfast?'

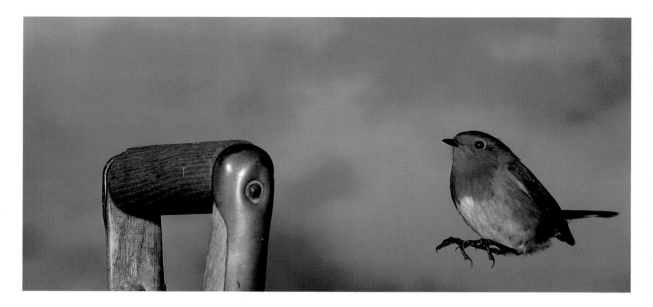

unsuitable for photography. So, we asked ourselves one day, is there any way we could manipulate the boundary – literally move the edge of the territory – to bring the dispute into a photogenically congenial area? Frustrated at our lack of success in filming territorial disputes, we cooked up a scheme of such fiendish cunning that it could only be a magnificent success or a dismal failure. We decided to bring two neighbouring robins into dispute at a place of *our* choosing by feeding them individually with mealworms, and then gradually moving the two mealworm supplies, and thus the two birds, closer together. To complete the ruse, we had another trick up our sleeve, for we had deliberately put netting over a berry-laden pyracantha, which was close to their territorial boundary, so that there was another food supply for whichever bird successfully laid claim to the bush. The bush was mostly in shadow during November and December, so we decided to wait for a higher sun in late January. Theory: once the mealworm supply is withdrawn and the netting removed from the berry-laden bush, birds will perform as required. Reality: by mid-January, the two robins turned out to be a male and a female, for they paired up leaving the bush in the *middle* of their territory. We were not as heartbroken as might have been expected, since, in the meantime, chaffinches and other enterprising birds had got under the netting and devoured most of the berries.

Compared with these tricks and stratagems, you might think that nest-photography would be straightforward. Not quite, as the

It is amazing what the camera reveals sometimes. Who would have thought that a robin could fly with its wings closed? Obviously the wings close to reduce drag and so prevent stalling in the split-second before landing.

120

following notes, taken from Mike's notebook, demonstrate. It is 3 March; Mike has set up a tray of tempting mealworms and a convenient perch near the kettle nest. His notes begin optimistically:

> I was preparing to photograph courtship feeding. I could see the male, who was constantly seeking mealworms, and the female, who was giving the 'feed me' call in the hedge. After completing the setting up of flash guns and re-baiting the tray, I returned indoors to the camera and within two minutes had successfully photographed the two birds on the perch engaged in courtship feeding. The flash and camera noise, however, made the female 'perch shy', and courtship feeding did not take place on that perch again that day, although both birds frequently visited it and fed from the tray. At times, while the female was there, she would sometimes give the 'feed me' call, but the lazy male just allowed her to feed herself.

On 4 March, our hero is up and ready for action by 6.30am:

> I connected flashes to the battery and set them up. The female was calling in the hedge and the male was constantly flitting around her. I baited the tray but before I could plug the flash lead into the camera, courtship feeding was taking place on the perch. Fortunately, it happened twice more and I had finished setting up and was able to photograph the second of these. Again the female took fright and courtship feeding took place elsewhere for the rest of my morning watch, which finished at 10.30.

His notes conclude:

> After that, although both birds continued to feed independently at the tray, all their courtship feeding took place away from the perch.

So, given that you have an abiding love for and interest in wildlife, what makes a good wildlife photographer? First of all, although it is something that takes a long time to learn, you have to accept that there are very few easy shots, even with a bird as tame and confiding as the robin. Some of the photographs in this book were straightforward, but many hours, even days, of work went into some of the individual shots. Add to that all the lost shots that did not quite come off (the robins' use of eyeshadow, recounted in Chapter 1, is a good example of the beautiful shot beautifully ruined), like the cat that comes around the corner and scares the birds off just when they were about to do whatever it was you wanted to capture on film. Then there are those throat-constricting moments familiar to all photographers when the subject is doing just what it should be doing, but you are not: you have looked away, you are changing films, you are just making a note in your notebook . . .

Secondly, you need to have a good eye for composition and to develop technique if you are going to make it as a photographer. How much of good photography is luck? Well, there are some occasions when only luck can help you, but even when Fate decides to offer you a rare gem, as in one classic shot of a jay photographed in the action of flying off with a stolen egg, you will still need all your photographic skills to take advantage of it. The fact is that good photography comes from a mixture of technique and a feeling for your subject. Decisions about composition, about the kind of lighting, the angle of lighting (sun over the shoulder or back-lighting the subject), about shutter speed – all these are important, and often have to be made very quickly, instinctively even.

There is one more ingredient. It is widely assumed that wildlife photographers must be people who have lots of patience. We are convinced – as are our friends and loved ones – that what we exhibit is not patience but persistence, the sheer dogged determination not to be beaten, not to give up, above all not to be satisfied until we have got the perfect shot. Which of course we never do, and never will: what matters is to keep on striving for that best shot, that perfect combination of light and mood and frame that encapsulates the subject and says, at last, everything that can be said about it.

There are still so many shots that we have yet to achieve. We still have not captured fighting robins on film, for instance, despite the fact that they do it so much. Skirmishes, though, are usually very brief and happen at such a speed and in so many locations around a territory that is has been impossible to record this dramatic event. Then we desperately wanted to show a parent bird plunging her head down between her chicks to peck at the nest-lining, but how on earth do you capture that? What we will say is that, for all the frustrations and disappointments and all the manifestations of Murphy's Law ('If something can go wrong, it will') during the robin project, we never lost our affection and our respect for these delightful little birds nor our enthusiasm for trying to reveal through photography the secrets and the surprises of their lives.

This final picture in our account of the robin is, fittingly, a portrait of Tame. Without his cooperation, we would have missed some fine shots. The angle of lighting as the sun goes down gives this picture a special quality. The last rays of the setting sun highlight Tame's red breast, and the yellowing evening light adds further mood and colour.

Bibliography

There are two books that are essential reading for anyone interested in finding out more about robins. First, there is the classic study by David Lack: *The Life of the Robin* (4th edn, Witherby, 1965). Unlike so many serious scientific monographs, it is highly readable and filled with literary allusions as well as with the results of scientific research. It is also a model of how to carry out and describe a field study. It is not surprising that everyone writing about robins will quote Lack before long. The other is Chris Mead's *Robins*, one of a series of delightful books published by Whittet Books. Chris Mead's book, like the others in the series, is packed with serious and important information presented in an accessible way and illustrated by witty line drawings. Although Chris Mead is probably at his happiest talking about ringing and migration, he has much to say about every aspect of the robin's life, and has used a great deal of information collected by the BTO to do so.

We referred to a number of texts for particular aspects, including:

General

Cramp, S. (ed.) *The Birds of the Western Palearctic*, Vol. 5 (Oxford University Press, 1988)

Hollom, P. A. D. *The Popular Handbook of British Birds*, 5th edn (Witherby, 1988)

Howard, R. & Moore, A. *A Complete Checklist of the Birds of the World* (Oxford University Press, 1980)

Nicholson, E. M. *Birds and Men*, New Naturalist Series (Collins, 1951)

Robertson, A. W. P. *Birds Wild and Free* (Bodley Head, 1950)

Simson, C. *A Bird Overhead* (London, 1966)

White, G. *The Natural History of Selborne* (Walter Scott, 1910)

Witherby, H. F. *et al. Handbook of British Birds* vols 1–5, 9th edn (Witherby, 1943)

Song

Armstrong, E. A. *A Study of Bird Song* (Dover, 1973)

Territory

Howard, E. *Territory in Birdlife* (Collins Fontana, 1964)

Nests and nest-finding

Atkinson, Rev. J. C. *British Birds, Eggs and Nests Popularly Described* (Routledge, 1870)

Campbell, B. & Ferguson-Lees, J. *A Field Guide to Birds' Nests* (Constable, 1972)

Harrison, C. *A Field Guide to the Nests, Eggs and Nestlings of British and European Birds* (Collins, 1975)

Mayer-Gross, H. *Nest Record Scheme* (BTO Guide No. 12, 1970)

Distribution

Lack, P. (ed.) *The Atlas of Wintering Birds in Britain and Ireland* (Poyser, 1986)

Sharrock, J. T. R. *The Atlas of Breeding Birds in Britain and Ireland* (Poyser, 1976)

Ageing and sexing

Svensson, L. *Identification Guide to European Passerines*, 3rd edn (Svensson, Stockholm, 1984. UK distributor: BTO)

Moult

Ginn, H. B. & Melville, D. S. *Moult in Birds* (BTO Guide No. 19, 1983)

Names and legends connected with Robins

Greenoak, F. *All the Birds of the Air* (André Deutsch, 1979)

Lockwood, W. B. *Oxford Book of British Bird Names* (Oxford University Press, 1984)

Photography

Hosking, E. *An Eye for a Bird* (Hutchinson/Arrow Books, 1973)

We also quoted from a number of magazine articles:

BBC Wildlife:
Gross, R. 'The kingfisher's sidekick' (December 1987, pp. 658–60)

British Birds:
May 1979: 'Robin with appearance of red-flanked bluetail'
October 1979: 'Avian orientation and navigation'
February 1980: 'Another aberrant robin resembling red-flanked bluetail'
February 1982: 'Feeding association between mole and birds'
November 1984: 'Robin eating gilled fungus'
August 1985: 'Pallas's warbler in October 1982' (quoting fall of robins on Isle of Man)

And from the following field guides:
Bruun, B. & Singer, A. *The Hamlyn Guide to Birds of Britain and Europe*, revised edn (Hamlyn, 1978)
Falla, R. A., Sibson, R. B. & Turbott, E. G. *The New Guide to the Birds of New Zealand* (Collins, 1983)
Maluquer i Sostres, J. *Els Ocells de les Terres Catalanes* (Barcino, 1973)
Perrins, C. *New Generation Guide to the Birds of Britain and Europe* (Collins, 1987)
Peterson, R., Mountford, G. & Hollom, P. A. D. *A Field Guide to the Birds of Britain and Europe*, 4th edn (Collins, 1983).
Peterson, R., Mountfort, G. & Hollom, P. A. D. *Guia de Campo de las Aves de Espana y de Europa* (Omega, 1973)
Simpson, K. & Day, N. *Field Guide to the Birds of Australia* (Croom Helm, 1989)

General Index

Numbers in **bold** refer to colour illustrations.

Index of Other Bird Species